Your 401k:

The Danger Within

Roger Levy

and

Peter Roland

Dedication

This guide is dedicated to the hard working men and women of America. We hope that this guide inspires you to provide adequately for many years of retirement when you are no longer receiving a paycheck!

ISBN-13: 978-1530672448

ISBN-10: 1530672449

Review

"An excellent guide! I wish I had it when I started at CEFEX!"

Carlos Panksep, Managing Director, the Centre for Fiduciary Excellence - CEFEX

Acknowledgment

We would like to thank the following people and organizations for their contributions to this book:

Patricia Webb of Canon Capital Investment Advisory *for her extensive technical knowledge, experience and insight from working with retirement plan sponsors and participants, as well as for her overall assistance with this guide.*

Vincent Daily *for his project management planning, creative consulting, and technical consulting.*

Francesco Galati *for his graphic design contributions and creative consulting.*

We encourage you to join America's Retirement Plan Coalition (ARPC) through our social media at:

https://www.linkedin.com/groups/2501193

https://twitter.com/AmericaRPC

Foreword to the Guide

February 29, 2016

Does your 401(k) plan offer the investment options and features that are best suited to provide you with a secure retirement income? The danger that may lurk within your plan is that available options are imprudent and that you are paying excessive expenses that eat away at investment earnings. This guide brings a novel approach to help you answer that question.

Employers have many responsibilities to meet before employees enroll in a 401(k) plan and many of these continue throughout the life of the plan. As a participant, you generally see only the results of your employer's decisions. The process your employer undertakes in making those decisions is rarely described. Yet if the employer's process were more transparent, you would have better tools to evaluate your plan and available investment options, building more confidence in the process. On the other hand, if you saw opportunities for improvement in the plan, you could bring these to your employer's attention.

Within this guide, you will follow the prudent steps that your employer should take in managing a 401(k) plan's investment process, with easy questions to ask your employer if any of these matters are unclear to you or seem amiss.

The foregoing matters are described in Part One of this guide. In Part Two, you will learn the basics of financial and retirement planning. Of necessity, this includes discussion of some of the material found in Part One, in case a reader should skip to Part Two first. In addition, because this guide may find its way into the hands of employers, there is a Message to Employers at the end of the guide, to explain the relevance of this guide to employers' fiduciary responsibilities.

Finally, while the guide refers to 401(k) plans, it applies equally to work-place 403(b) plans!

Table of Contents

Introduction

Employers today are doing more than ever to help employees provide for their retirement.[1] Much of the effort focuses on maximizing the savings and investment opportunities offered by the company 401(k) plan. This is a welcome development.

However, much of what drives participant investment outcomes is based on decisions made by employers, yet participants are largely ignorant of how those decisions are made. This lack of transparency is detrimental. If participants had a better understanding of how the architecture of their plan was determined, investment outcomes could well improve and the need for regulatory investigations and fiduciary breach lawsuits might diminish.

The purpose of this guide is to educate 401(k) plan participants on those attributes of a retirement plan which can have long term influence over their retirement income prospects, but which are largely under the control of their employer and go unexplained in materials provided to participants upon enrollment or subsequently in annual reports.

Then, having explained these important architectural attributes, we'll provide some general financial planning tips and guidance on personal asset allocation and the decisions participants face when they leave their employment.

Background

Participants in 401(k) plans have access to multiple resources to help them develop retirement income security. Enrollment materials explain how the plan operates, the benefits of tax deferred investment earnings, how to maximize employer contributions (if available under the plan), the investment fund choices, and how to make contribution and investment elections.

Subsequent investment education will explain the value of starting contributions early in one's career, the benefits of compound returns, how the economy and capital markets work, the need for investment diversification, and how investments can be optimally allocated among fund choices, taking into account one's age and risk tolerance. Quarterly and annual disclosures inform participants about investment earnings and expenses charged to their account and may also provide a projection of the retirement income that a participant may expect, based on the participant's continued contributions and investment earnings.

In some instances, employers may offer participants access to personalized investment advice. All of this is designed to help participants generate the retirement income they will need when their working career is over.

It takes a lot of manpower and expense to support this education effort and one has to question whether the effort is worth it, because the evidence suggests that participants make poor decisions in saving for retirement. The evidence, in part, lies in comparing the investment performance of professionally managed defined benefit (DB) plans with the investment performance of participant-directed defined contribution (DC) plans, which include 401(k) plans. For example, a 2006 study performed by the Center for Retirement Research at Boston College found that, over the period 1988-2004, DB plans outperformed 401(k) plans by one percentage point (Investment Returns: Defined Benefit VS. 401(k) Plans, Munnell, Soto, Libby and Prinzivalli, September 2006). That may not seem like a lot, but $50,000 invested for 25 years at 7% will earn $57,000 more than if the investment were made at 6%. So the difference is important.

Similar findings appear in other studies. For example, Towers Watson, looking at 2000 plans for 2011 found that the median investment return for DB plans was 2.74%, while the median investment return for DC plans was -0.22% (Tower Watson, July 2013). Dalbar, using a different approach and examining the behavior of "average investors", found that, in 2014, the 20 year annualized return of the S&P was 9.58% while the 20 year annualized return for the average equity mutual fund investor was only 5.19%, a gap of 4.66%. Their conclusion? Despite the efforts of industry experts, investor imprudence continues to be widespread (Dalbar: 21st Annual Quantitative Analysis of Investor Behavior). This seems to be supported by the results of a 2015 survey conducted by Lincoln Financial Group which found that, while 81% of Americans are optimistic about their financial future, only 66% consider themselves prepared for retirement (Measuring Optimism, Outlook, and Direction, Lincoln Financial Group, 2015).

Against this background, we want to direct the attention of 401(k) plan participants to the role that their employers play in adopting and managing the many plan features that have such an important impact on a participant's ability to save for retirement.

For example, we have already mentioned the manpower and expense associated with investment education and disclosures. Do plan participants understand that the cost of this pretty much comes out of their pockets? If they were to recognize this, they could be motivated to do one of two things: they could say, if we're paying for it, we may as well take advantage of it; or, they could say that the money is wasted, that education efforts should be curtailed and that the resulting savings should go into their account, a win either way. In our view, participants are entitled to greater transparency on these and other issues than currently exists.

Rules that Govern Retirement Plans

The rules that govern 401(k) plans were designed pretty much with traditional pension plans in mind. Put simply, in a traditional pension plan, the employer promises to pay retirement benefits to its employees and is then responsible for making sure that there is enough money to pay those benefits when due. Also, the employer bears all the investment fees and the costs of administration. Thus, with a pension plan, the rules governing employer duties regarding contributions, prudent investing, and paying only reasonable costs, are of little concern to employees. However well or badly the employer performs or complies with government rules, it doesn't much matter to the employees because they have the employer's promise to pay, win, lose or draw. Furthermore, they can fall back on the Pension Benefit Guaranty Corporation if the employer falls down. They are there to back up broken employer promises.

Not so with a 401(k) plan, where the employee is responsible for making his or her own contributions, for managing his/her own investment account, and, often times, for paying the investment fees and administration costs. Yet, it is the employer who picks the funds and service providers and who determines how much and in what manner fees and expenses should be paid. Certainly, the employer remains subject to strict rules of conduct on these matters, but the process adopted by the employer for dealing with these matters remains as opaque as if the plan were a traditional pension plan. And oh, by the way, there is no support from the Pension Benefit Guaranty Corporation if a participant loses money in his/her 401(k) account or if a participant's savings are insufficient to replace lost wages!

To the extent that transparency does occur regarding the process followed by an employer, it is often as a result of government investigation or lawsuits. That seems to us to be a costly and unnecessary road to participant enlightenment.

This guide is not intended to be a discussion of the law applicable to 401(k) plans, but some mention of the law is necessary if only to support some of our contentions. 401(k) plans are governed by the Employee Retirement Income Security Act of 1974, which among other things lays down the responsibilities of loyalty and care that those managing a retirement plan owe to participants and beneficiaries. These responsibilities are known as "fiduciary'" responsibilities. Now, the word "fiduciary" causes the eyes of some people to glaze over or their heads to roll back with their eyes star ward. But, fiduciary responsibilities are too important to ignore or, for employers, to shirk, although a recent study shows that one third of employers don't realize that they are fiduciaries, an increase of 7% since 2011.[2] But for participants, the notion of "fiduciary responsibility" should be seen as a positive attribute of 401(k) participation. For, it represents the source of much needed protection, however much employers might choose to ignore it.

For our purposes, a "fiduciary" is a person who is responsible for managing someone else's money and therefore holds a special position of trust and confidence towards that someone else. That trust and confidence gives rise to specific responsibilities. These "fiduciary" responsibilities are principally concerned with duties of care and loyalty owed to those to whom the money ultimately belongs.[3] In a 401(k) plan, the employer, sometimes called the plan sponsor, is a fiduciary because the employer acts as a steward of your interests as a participant and, as such, generally manages the selection of the funds in which you invest, while also performing other functions. For example, the employer may also appoint an investment committee and/or an investment adviser to oversee fund selection and replacement. If so, each committee member and the adviser will likely be a fiduciary, too.

With that understanding, let's take a quick look at a recent case before the U.S. Supreme Court. In *Tibble v. Edison, Int'l*, 135 S. Ct. 1823, (2015), the U.S. Supreme Court said that, in considering the contours of fiduciary duty, the courts must often look at the law of trusts, and the Court proceeded to apply trust law to a failure by those managing a 401(k) plan to monitor investments once selected.

Looking elsewhere at the law of trusts, the Restatement (Second) of Trusts[4] would impose, on employers, a duty to communicate to participants any material facts affecting their interests which employers know that the participants don't know, and which the participants need to know for their protection. We believe that much of what they discuss in this guide falls within the scope of this duty because what, as a steward of your interests, your employer is not telling you about the investment process your employer has adopted is material, it affects your interests in the plan, and you have a need to know in order to protect those interests.

In any event, we believe that the transparency advocated within these pages represents a prudent practice that all employers should come to adopt. Some will say that 401(k) plan participants are already overloaded with information that is hard to absorb and that more information will increase confusion. To this one must say that the information currently deprived from participants is the information participants need to evaluate the quality and suitability of their 401(k) plan. With this gap filled, we believe that participants will be better prepared for the decisions they must make.

Then, there is the question of trust. According to a survey published by the American Psychological Association in 2014[5], nearly 1 in 4 workers say they don't trust their employer and only about half believe their employer is open and upfront with them. While the survey did not focus on satisfaction with the company retirement plan, it may be that employee trust would improve if employers were more open about how they manage the company 401(k) plan and if they provided broader disclosure of their investment process.

With the foregoing in mind, this guide is intended to assist you in reaching your retirement income goals. It should be noted that the content is not a comprehensive financial planning guide, but a basic framework to assist you in making better decisions with regard to your 401(k) plan. So, if you, the reader, are a participant in a 401(k) plan, treat this guide as a companion to your enrollment material and annual reports. Each chapter starts with the topics about which you will learn and ends with questions you may ask your employer if your knowledge about a specific topic is incomplete. It is suggested that you should accumulate your questions as you go through the guide and review what you have accumulated before going to your employer. Employers have been trained to believe that ERISA defines the limits of their obligations and so may be surprised to receive questions about their role as fiduciaries. With this in mind, you may even choose to share this guide with your employer. Apart from anything else, it may encourage your employer to seek ways to improve your plan, should that opportunity exist.

Structure of this Guide

Part 1	Part 2
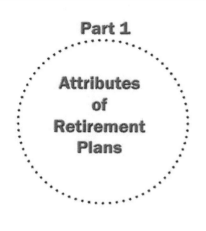	

Attributes of Retirement Plans

Personal Financial Planning Including Retirement Plans

[1] JP Morgan, Aligning goals, improving outcomes, 2015 Defined Contribution Plan Sponsor Survey Findings

[2] Inside the Minds of Plan Sponsors, Alliance Bernstein, 2015

[3] Note that until a participant becomes entitled to a distribution, the plan holds the assets in trust. Generally, participants become entitled to a distribution: upon death, disability or severance from employment; plan termination; or upon reaching age 59 ½ or incurring financial hardship. (26 CFR 1.401(k)-1(d)(3))

[4] Comment d to section 173 of the *Restatement (Second) of Trusts* provides:

Ordinarily the trustee is not under a duty to the beneficiary to furnish in- formation to him in the absence of a request for such information . . . . In dealing with the beneficiary on the trustee's own account, however, he is under a duty to communicate to the beneficiary all material facts in connection with the transaction which the trustee knows or should know . .

. . Even if the trustee is not dealing with the beneficiary on the trustee's own account, he is under a duty to communicate to the beneficiary material facts affecting the interest of the beneficiary which he knows the beneficiary does not know and which the beneficiary needs to know for his protection in dealing with a third person . . . .

[5] American Psychological Association's 2014 Work and Well-Being Survey, April 23, 2014 http://www.apaexcellence.org/assets/general/2014-work-and- wellbeing-survey-results.pdf

Chapter 1: Plan Fees

What you will learn:

1. **It costs money to participate in a 401K plan – Yes, you are charged fees for participating!**
2. **Why knowing about fees is important**
3. **What kind of fees you will pay**
4. **What range of fees to expect**
5. **Your employer's responsibilities**
6. **Questions to ask your employer**

1. It costs money to participate in a 401K plan – Yes, you are charged fees for participating!

Writing of the permanency of the Constitution in 1789, Benjamin Franklin said "…but in this world nothing can be said to be certain, except death and taxes." Franklin clearly was not a participant in a 401K plan! Now, we have death, taxes, and 401(k) plan fees!

As mentioned in the Introduction, when you join a 401K plan you receive an enrollment kit which tells you all about the plan, the investment options available to you and how to elect contributions and select the funds in which you want to invest. There will also be some guidance on building a portfolio based on your risk tolerance and your age. Until 2012, when the US Department of Labor (DOL) issued new regulation to broaden the scope and frequency of fee disclosures, enrollment kits barely mentioned the cost associated with being a 401K participant. Today, you'll find the disclosures in the enrollment kits but in many cases the disclosures are tucked away in fine print after all the benefits of participating have been highlighted. So, it is little wonder that participants are largely ignorant of the cost of being in a 401K plan when they join, and the participant uprising against the high cost of 401K participation, anticipated from the 2012 DOL introduction of new quarterly and annual disclosures, never materialized. In fact, some participants still believe that participation is either free or is paid for by their employers. What's worse, this has led to some plans continuing to pay excessive fees.

However, excessive 401K fees did not slip the attention of the class action bar who, around 2006, began a spate of lawsuits against some household name companies alleging fiduciary breach for charging 401K participants excessive fees. Early suits against United Technologies, Unisys, Honda of America, Deere, AG Edwards, and others were dismissed, but suits against Lockheed Martin, International Paper, General Dynamics, Kraft Foods, Caterpillar, ABB, and Bechtel, for example, resulted in damage awards or settlements favorable to the participants. Another case, Tibble v. Edison went to the US Supreme Court in 2014 and is now remanded for further proceedings.

2. Why knowing about fees is important

The answer is simple. However much you grow the assets in your account, the growth is going to be reduced every year by fees charged to your account. The higher the fees, the lower the growth.

An illustration may help.

Take someone with an account balance of $25,000 which grows over 25 years at 7%. If the participant bears expenses of 0.50% each year, the account balance at the end of 25 years will be $120,690. However, if the average expenses were 1.50%, at the end of 25 years, the account would only be worth $95,335, a difference of $25,355!

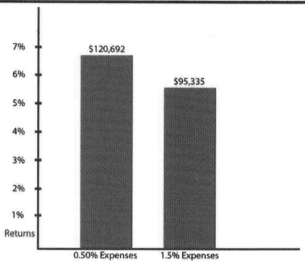

$25,000 invested for 25 Years at 7%

Looked at from a different perspective, whether you're an investment guru or a novice, every year, expenses will eat away at your retirement savings no matter how good or bad your investment strategy. Like death and taxes, 401k expenses are inevitable! When we talk about "fees" and "expenses", bear in mind that the regulators, the US Department of Labor, and industry professionals, use the words "fees" and "expenses" interchangeably. So, we will inevitably do likewise, even though you could draw a distinction between them.

3. What kind of fees you will pay

Fees fall into (3) general categories: plan administration expenses, investment fees and transaction service fees.

Types of Plan Fees

◦ Plan Administration Expenses ◦

◦   Investment Fees   ◦

◦ Transaction and Service Fees ◦

Let's look at these categories:

Plan Administration Expenses

The operation of a 401k plan is fairly complex and may involve a number of different service providers, all of whom may be paid out of plan assets, i.e. participant accounts, unless the employer opts to pay them, which tends to be rare. The operation of a plan includes recordkeeping, administration (sometimes bundled with recordkeeping), trustee/custodian services (holding the assets) legal and accounting, access to customer service representatives, educational seminars and material, enrollment services, daily valuation of plan investments, processing transactions and, maybe, participant investment advice.

When administration expenses are charged against the plan, they may be charged as a flat fee per participant or pro rata, that is in proportion to each account balance. Of course, if charged pro rata, participants with the larger balances bear more of the cost. The likelihood of fees being charged pro rata increases when there is "revenue sharing", an arrangement with an investment provider under which a portion of

13

investment fees charged to each account is allocated to administrations costs and is paid to the appropriate service provider. You'll find a more detailed discussion of revenue sharing in the next chapter.

Investment Fees

Managing plan investments incurs a fee and other expenses. Generally, these take the form of asset based fees (i.e. a percentage of the assets), typically included in the "expense ratio" charged by the investment provider, such as a mutual fund or a collective investment trust. Investment fees are usually the largest component of 401K plan fees and expenses. You need to pay attention to these fees as they may vary from fund to fund within the choices you are offered. Also, they are an indirect charge against your account in that they are deducted from the investment returns before the returns are credited to your account. In other words, investment returns are reported net of investment fees and so, unless you look for investment fees in the disclosures you receive, you won't know what you are paying. They may also be referred to as "Total Operating Expenses." Note also that you may be charged for fees paid to an investment advisor hired by the plan to help with selection of the fund choices.

Transaction and Service Fees

In addition to general administration expenses, a plan will charge participants fees for certain transactions, such as loan processing or dealing with a Qualified Domestic Relations Order (QDRO). Such fees are a fixed amount.

4. The range of fees to expect

Participant fees will vary based on the number of participants, the volume of assets and the services provided, such as participant education. Small plans inevitably have a higher cost per participant than large plans because there is a certain cost threshold for administration and that cost per participant will be higher if there are 10 participants than if there are 2,000.

According to the 401k Averages Book (15th edition), in a plan with 10 participants and $500,000 in assets, a participant will pay, on average, $953 per year in administration and investment expenses, of which the investment expense represents 78%, resulting in the investment expense being 1.48% of assets. In contrast, in a plan with 2,000 participants and $20,000,000 in assets, a participant will pay, on average, $127 per year in administration and investment expenses, of which the investment expense represents 87%, resulting in the investment expense being 1.10% of assets. A significant difference when applied over 25 years.

Number of Participants	Total Plan Assets	Average Per Participant Cost	Percent of cost Attributable to Investment Expense	Investment Expense as Percentage of Assets
10	$500,000	$953	78%	1.48%
2,000	$20,000,000	$127	87%	1.1%

5. Your employer's responsibilities

Clearly, scale has a lot to do with what you pay and so expect your cost of participation in a 401K plan to be higher if you work for a small company. With that understanding, small companies should pay very careful attention to cost when they select plan service providers. As we have seen with prior examples, a 1% per annum difference in expenses can have a significant negative impact on a $25,000 account balance over 25 years, reducing it from $120,000 to $95,000. However, large companies are not immune to overpaying, and so even if you work at a Fortune 500 Company, you need to examine what you are paying.

Irrespective of the size of your employer, most likely, your employer has been diligent in selecting and monitoring service providers and has made prudent choices, which is an employer's fiduciary responsibility, but there is no reason why you cannot ask your employer about this. Bear in mind, that your employer is not bound to select the cheapest provider. For example, if an employer decides that the quality of services of provider "A" is superior to that of Provider "B", the employer may select "A" even if "B" is cheaper. The employer must determine that, taken together, the services and cost of a provider are reasonable. So this is not a black and white issue.

In terms of other responsibilities, once a service provider has been prudently selected, your employer should periodically monitor the provider's services and costs. There is no fixed rule for this type of monitoring but, today, employers have access to published data, like the 401k Averages Book, and an annual review would be appropriate. Certainly, no more than 3 to 5 years should pass without a full evaluation using a competitive bidding process. With all of that in mind, here are some questions to ask your employer if you are unsure of your plan fee arrangements:

6. Questions to ask your employer

1. Who are the plan's service providers and how did you select them?
2. Did you conduct any competitive bidding? For example, did you issue an RFP - Request for Proposal?
3. If no competitive bidding occurred, how did you evaluate the services and cost of the provider(s) you selected?
4. For how long have the service providers been under contract with the plan?

5. How often do you review service provider arrangements for sufficiency and reasonableness?

6. Do you benchmark service provider fees? If so, how often?

7. When was the last time a competitive bidding process was conducted?

8. Are we paying for services we don't use?

9. Are any service provider fees paid by the Company and, if so, how much and for what?

10. How much are the participants paying and is this charged to participants as a flat fee or pro rata?

Chapter 2: Understanding Investment Fees

What you will learn:

1. The components of mutual fund fees
2. How "revenue sharing" works
3. The importance of fund share class selection
4. How other investment vehicles charge fees
5. Hidden fees
6. Summary
7. Your employer's responsibilities
8. Questions to ask your employer

Introduction

Knowing that any charge for fees and expenses against your account reduces the growth of your investments, it is clearly important to keep those charges to a minimum. To a certain extent, you are at the mercy of your employer, because it is they who are responsible for the initial fund selection and for then monitoring the funds on a periodic basis, to ensure that the funds remain suitable investments. As a 401(k) participant, you need to do your own monitoring: otherwise, you won't know what you're paying for or whether the cost is reasonable.

To conduct effective monitoring, you need to understand how investment fees and expenses work.

More than 60% of 401(k) assets are invested in mutual funds.[6] The balance is invested in a variety of different vehicles, such as: collective investment trusts (CITs), insurance company guaranteed investment contracts (GICs), separate accounts, Exchange Traded Funds (ETFs) and group variable annuity contracts. These vehicles all charge fees and expenses, but there are differences, which we will highlight.

Let's start with mutual funds since they are the most common.

1. The components of mutual fund fees

Investing in mutual funds through your 401(k) may involve two types of fees: sales loads, which are one time fees, and recurring fees (expense ratio).

Sales loads are charged either when you first invest (front-end loads) or when you redeem or sell your shares (back-end loads). Either way, they are not a good thing and are to be avoided. For example, front-end loads can be as much as 5.75% on the first $25,000 of investment with additional investment being subject to a declining load until $1 million is invested, when the load disappears. Fortunately, front- end sales loads are almost always waived for 401(k) plans, but 14% of all 401(k) mutual fund assets are invested in load funds.[7] This may result from the use of a plan feature known as a "brokerage window", which allows participants to use a retail brokerage account to purchase investments not offered as part of a plan's core investment funds. We'll speak more of brokerage windows later, but you need to be aware of sales loads, nonetheless.

Recurring fees take the form of an "expense ratio".

What is in a fund's "expense ratio"?

The expense ratio is a fee charged by a fund as a percentage of the assets it holds and the amount will depend in part on the type of fund involved. Index funds tend to be the least expensive on average, (0.70%), followed by actively managed bond funds, (0.98%), with actively managed equity funds, (1.33%), being the most expensive as of the end of 2014.[8]

Expense Ratio for Selected Investment Objectives

Index Equity Funds	Bond Funds	Managed Equity Funds
0.70%	0.98%	1.33%

The following identifies the components of the expense ratio:

- **Investment management fee**

  A fund has a board of directors and one of their functions is to establish the fee which the fund pays for investment management, usually to a separate investment advisory firm. The management fee includes compensation for the portfolio manager and staff, operations, investment research, and expenses incurred in relation to investment decisions.

- **Administrative Expense**

  The expense ratio will also include a portion to cover the fund's costs of registration as a mutual fund, regulatory compliance, customer service, producing fund prospectuses, mailings and the like.

- **Revenue Sharing**

  Revenue sharing occurs when a mutual fund allocates part of the expense ratio to pay other providers for services they perform for the plan. A mutual fund predetermines how much it will add to the expense ratio for this purpose. Revenue sharing is paid out in the form of fees permitted by the SEC. Being part of the expense ratio, these fees reduce the returns which are credited to your account as a 401(k) plan participant and they are deducted before investment performance is reported. So you have a natural interest in what is being charged and what it is used for, as discussed below.

2. How "Revenue Sharing" works

We briefly described in the last bullet point how revenue sharing works and we will develop this theme below, but, first, what is its purpose? In a nutshell, *revenue sharing is a method of using investment fees received from plan participants to pay plan service providers for administration and other services without participants seeing a direct charge to their account.*

The following explains what is paid out as fees by the mutual fund from the expense ratio as revenue sharing:

- **12b-1 Distribution Fees**

  Named after the 1980 SEC rule which authorized them, 12b-1 fees are intended to cover the costs of marketing and selling fund shares. In practice, they are applied by brokers and advisers for services they provide to the plan, such as selecting and monitoring the mutual funds, conducting enrollment meetings, and providing participants with investment education.

- **Shareholder Servicing Fees and Sub-transfer Agency Fees**

  These fees are intended to pay 401(k) plan recordkeepers for keeping track of share ownership by the plan and participants on an omnibus account basis, thereby relieving the fund of this function. In practice they are applied towards the general cost of plan recordkeeping and administration services. Payments may cover the entire cost of what the recordkeeper would otherwise charge the plan. If not, the service provider will bill your plan for the excess cost and you may see a direct charge to your account.

The justification offered for revenue sharing is that it facilitates payment for some or all of the recordkeeping and administrative services necessary for the proper running of a 401(k) plan, but critics say that it is a mechanism to pay undisclosed and conflicted compensation. For example, the availability of revenue sharing could encourage investment advisers to recommend only funds that offer the highest level of revenue sharing. Alternatively, a recordkeeper whose reasonable cost of services is, say, $50,000, could receive more than that in revenue sharing as plan assets and revenue share both grow.

A further criticism of revenue sharing is that it can lead to unfair allocations between participants. As you will learn in the next section, the amount of revenue sharing available to a plan may vary from fund to fund. In other words, amounts made available for revenue sharing are not uniform, even among funds of the same family. Consider therefore what occurs when the amount available for revenue sharing differs among the funds available in your plan. Take the following, for example:

Fund A – Amount available for revenue sharing - 1%

Fund B – Amount available for revenue sharing – 0.75%

Fund C – Amount available for revenue sharing – 0.50%

Fund D – Amount available for revenue sharing – 0 – No revenue sharing

Fund E – Amount available for revenue sharing – 0 – No revenue sharing

If participant X invests in Funds A, B, and C, participant X will likely pay more of the administration expenses than Participant Y who invests in Funds C, D, and E.

So, is revenue sharing a good or a bad thing for you as a participant? The reality is that 401(k) plans are not free. Many people think of the cost of being in a 401(k) plan solely in terms of investment management fees, because that is what they are familiar with. But, as we have seen, there are many other services necessary in running a 401(k) plan that must be paid. Revenue sharing is a recognized way of meeting these additional expenses.

Your employer has to make a prudent decision about adopting revenue sharing and has to ensure that service providers are paid only what is reasonable and that you, as a participant, receive full disclosure of what is charged to your account, both directly and indirectly. If that occurs, revenue sharing is regarded as acceptable. However, many of the excessive fee, fiduciary breach lawsuits we have mentioned involved revenue sharing issues, thus placing revenue sharing in a poor light, even though the courts treat revenue sharing as acceptable.

In our opinion, revenue sharing, as it is currently implemented, lacks transparency and can lead to participants paying more in fees than is reasonable and to disparity in the way that expenses are shared among participants. Some suggest that fairness dictates that the amounts derived from revenue sharing, instead of being paid out to service providers, should be deposited back in the plan and be credited to the accounts of the participants whose investments generated the revenue sharing. Then the administration expenses would be charged to participants pro rata so that all participants pay their proportional costs of the plan. This is referred to as

"equalization". However, why bother? The same result would be achieved with greater transparency by simply eliminating revenue sharing and purchasing funds that don't include it. Of course, there is always an exception to the rule and, here, it is that, if your plan has under $1 million in assets, share classes that exclude revenue sharing may be unavailable and the use of a share class which includes revenue sharing may then be unavoidable. In that case, equalization would be a suitable technique to ensure reasonable fairness in the allocation of expenses and more record keepers are updating their systems to permit this.

You will want to examine what happens under your plan, so let's see how investment fees and expenses, including revenue sharing, may be charged.

3. The importance of fund share class selection

To learn about fund fees and expenses, participants are always told to read a fund's prospectus, a daunting task given the fine print and legalese. A potentially easier way to find out what you're paying is to identify a fund's share class.

Your plan invests in a mutual fund by buying shares from the fund. Mutual funds make available different share classes to meet different needs and circumstances. However, the underlying investments are identical in each case.

Share classes tend to be divided between retail and institutional share classes. Generally, retail class shares have sales charges, either front-end or back-end loads, as previously discussed. Institutional class shares, which are generally available only to retirement plans, do not.

Retail class shares tend to have a higher expense ratio than institutional class shares, but retail class shares are still found in 401(k) plans, even large ones, generally to support revenue sharing. This higher expense ratio is why there have been so many lawsuits over plans paying unnecessarily high fees.

The share class of each fund in your plan was selected by your employer and possibly, as a best practice, your employer had the help of an outside adviser. Curiously, though, when identifying the investment options in quarterly and annual disclosures which you receive from your plan, your employer is not required by DOL regulation to include the share class in the description. However, for mutual funds, the share class and associated expenses can be found in the fund prospectus you receive when you invest in a fund.

Let's now take a look at the different share classes. But be forewarned, the mutual fund industry has created an alphabet soup of share classes and the terms of each class may vary between fund families. The confusion serves to hide, some would say intentionally, compensation paid by the funds through revenue sharing.

"A" class shares

These shares incur a front-end sales charge or "load" which is a commission or sales charge applied at the time of purchase. These are almost always waived in a 401(k) plan for core investments, but, as we mentioned earlier, if your plan offers a brokerage window, funds purchased through that arrangement would not be immune from applicable retail sales loads.

With A class shares, the annual expense ratio will be in the range of 0.90%

"B" class shares

These shares incur no front–end load, but there may be a back-end load or deferred sales charge if you sell the shares within a specified holding period (e.g., 5 -10 years). If you maintain ownership beyond the initial holding period, the shares automatically convert to A class shares, with lower expense ratios. Again, these sales charges are generally waived in a 401(k) plan.

The annual expense ratio associated with B class shares will be in the range of 1.65% but will drop to 0.90% upon conversion to A shares.

"C" class shares

C class shares do not have a front-end load but generally have an annual 1% 12b-1 fee built into the expense ratio each year. There may be a back-end load which is waived after a certain holding period (one year, for example). The back-end load will likely be lower than with B class shares.

C class shares have a lower expense ratio than B class shares, but higher than A class shares.

"R" Class Shares

These shares are found only in retirement plans. They have no front-end or back-end loads and have lower expense ratios than retail share classes. Ideally, your plan should opt for R class shares for your plan but don't be surprised to find retail class shares. Despite the lower cost of R class shares, retail class shares appeal to some employers because, as we have previously stated, they afford the opportunity to pay for plan expenses through revenue sharing. To be sure, some fund families also offer different classes of R class shares to allow for revenue sharing even though the overall expense ratio is less than with retail class shares. Note that there are also "I" or "Y" class shares available to certain institutional investors that have no sales charges or 12b-1 fees.

An example may be helpful. Let's take the MFS Total Return Fund. This is available with 9 relevant share classes intended to meet different circumstances and needs. The following table illustrates the variations available:

Share Class	A	B	C	I	R1	R2	R3	R4	R5
Max Sales Charge	5.75%	None	None	None	None	None	None	None	None
Deferred Sales Charge	1.00%	4.00%	1.00%	None	None	None	None	None	None
Management Fee	0.35%	0.35%	0.35%	0.35%	0.35%	0.35%	0.35%	0.35%	0.35%
12b-1 Fees	0.25%	1.00%	1.00%	None	1.00%	0.50%	0.25%	None	None
Other Expenses	0.13%	0.13%	0.13%	0.13%	0.13%	0.13%	0.13%	0.13%	0.06%
Total Annual Operating Expenses	0.73%	1.48%	1.48%	0.48%	1.48%	0.98%	0.73%	0.48%	0.41%

As you can see from the table, Class A shares have a lower expense ratio (Total Annual Operating Expenses) than both the R1 and R2 share classes. The difference reflects that, even with institutional class shares, fund companies make some portion of their fees available for revenue sharing. Bear in mind, however, that not all R class shares are available to plans with less than $1 million in assets.

We mentioned in Chapter 1 the growing success of fiduciary breach lawsuits challenging employers who allow their 401(k) plans to charge excessive fees. There is growing evidence that the mutual fund industry, at least, is beginning to overhaul and rationalize share classes. According to a report in Planadviser[9],

60% of funds will make changes to share classes in 2016. Some will apparently add share classes with zero revenue share while others will eliminate share classes that allow revenue sharing. Employers and their advisers are hopefully paying attention.

Let's now look at other types of investment vehicles that may be used in your plan and the way that they charge fees.

4. How other investment vehicles charge fees

Collective Investment Trust Funds (CITs)

These funds, also called commingled investment funds, are established by a bank or trust company to pool the investments of multiple retirement plans, but not individual investors. Accordingly they are similar to mutual funds but are less expensive to establish and manage because they are subject to a different regulatory regime. Nevertheless, CITs have a similar fee structure to mutual funds with a specified expense ratio that includes asset management and administrative fees and potential revenue sharing. However, it should also be noted that they are harder for individuals to track because there is no public reporting or tracking available as there is with mutual funds

Insurance Company General Accounts

Investments in these accounts carry a promise of preservation of principal and a fixed or indexed rate of return. They are issued as Guaranteed Investment Contracts (GICs) and are backed by the general assets of the insurance company and are subject to their financial viability. The expenses related to managing the account are borne exclusively by the insurance company and so there is no prescribed expense ratio published. In other words, what remains after paying all guaranteed returns belongs to the insurance company and it pays its expenses from the balance of the income. Accordingly, there is no express expense ratio or reported investment fee.

Stable Value Funds

Stable value funds are created exclusively for 401(k) plans and other types of defined contribution plans and are designed to provide higher returns than a money market fund but with similar stability of principal. They consist of pooled or commingled funds which hold an underlying portfolio of high quality bonds secured by a "wrap" contract, a form of insurance, which ensures that participants can purchase and redeem their investments without bearing the impact of price fluctuations within the bond portfolios. In other words, when you invest $1 you can get $1 back without worrying whether any underlying investment has gone down in value and you earn a return while the $1 is invested.

Stable value funds are not organized as mutual funds but they have an expense ratio which works similarly to that of a mutual fund. So the stable value fund expense ratio includes allocations for investment management, insurance fees, administrative costs, and any revenue sharing built into the pricing.

Exchange Traded Funds (ETF's)

Exchange Traded Funds, or ETFs, have been around for a number of years but their use as 401(k) investment options has been more recent. So, what are they?

ETFs are a basket of securities that trade as a single security, like a regular stock on an exchange. Most ETFs are index funds and try to replicate the performance of a particular index, just like index mutual funds. However, the way that they are priced and traded differs from a mutual fund.

Mutual fund shares are purchased from and are redeemed by the issuing fund company and are priced at the fund's Net Asset

Value (NAV), which is established at the end of the day based on the closing price of the securities held by the fund.

In contrast, investors can generally buy and sell ETF's in the stock market at the intra-day market price, which can fluctuate during the day, just as with any stock. While the price generally reflects the price of the underlying securities, ETFs may be traded at a premium or discount reflecting market conditions. Being able to trade ETFs during the day appeals to some investors but when used as a fund choice in a 401(k) plan, that advantage will be unavailable. This is because most recordkeepers will pool purchases and sales across a plan and execute trades at the end of the day based on the net position. Since 401(k) investments are meant to be held long term and not traded frequently, this disadvantage should not be material.

ETFs are generally cheaper to own than mutual funds and offer greater transparency in that their holdings and expenses are visible at all times. This should appeal to employers and participants. However, not all record keeping firms have systems to accommodate their use.

Like mutual funds, ETFs incur an expense ratio but, unlike mutual funds, revenue sharing is unavailable as a means of paying 401(k) plan expenses, which may account for slower adoption by employers. According to Bloomberg, the average expense ratio of non-leveraged ETFs in 2014 was 0.50% but for managed ETFs the expense ratio was in the range of 1.50%.[10] However, trading ETFs incurs trading costs, such as brokerage commissions, the spread between bid and ask prices, and the difference between the ETF price and the value of underlying securities. But note that some service providers are able to offer commission free trading.

Group Variable Annuity Contracts

Many insurance companies offer variable annuity contracts to 401(k) plans. These act as a single funding vehicle, meaning that the insurance company holds all of the assets of the plan, partly in its general account, as discussed above, and partly in separate accounts which generally hold shares in mutual funds. These mutual funds will usually consist of a mix of proprietary funds, being those owned and managed by the insurance company, and non-proprietary funds, being other mutual funds or investment products. Another alternative is for the insurance company to use sub-advised funds. These are not mutual funds but pooled accounts designed to: (i) imitate the strategy of a particular mutual fund; and (ii) give the insurance company a degree of exclusivity in access to the pool.

So, if your employer has selected a variable annuity provider, you won't be able to check the price of your funds online or in a newspaper. That is because you don't own shares in those funds. You own a share, called a "unit", in an insurance company separate account which has purchased the mutual fund or pooled account shares on behalf of the plan.

Accordingly, in the case of mutual funds, you won't know the share class purchased by the insurance company or whether revenue sharing is involved. What you will be told is simply the annual operating expenses of each separate account which may be as much as 0.84% to 1.36% in a small plan with, say, under $500,000 in assets.

Variable annuity contracts have many layers of fees in addition to the investment fees just discussed. Typically these will include one or more of the following expenses:

Variable Asset Charge to pay the insurance company for general administration, recordkeeping, participant services and commissions paid to the broker/agent who sold the plan to your employer.

Insurance related charges, sometimes called "Mortality and Expense" or "M&E" to cover the cost of insurance features within the variable annuity contract, such as an annuity or guaranteed lifetime income stream, interest and expense guarantees, and any death benefit available under the contract.

Surrender Charges payable if the employer terminates the contract before a specific time period expires. These charges will likely scale down over time.

Suffice it to say that a participant's cost of being invested under a group variable annuity contract is likely to be higher than being invested in mutual funds directly. This is by virtue of the additional expenses identified above which, apart from surrender charges, can amount to 1.85% annually in small plans. Added to fund expense ratios between 0.84% and 1.36%, you can end up paying over 3% in expenses every year.

However, there are group annuity contracts available today in which some or all of these expenses are reduced or stripped out so that the cost of being in a group annuity contract is comparable to being in a plan which invests directly in mutual funds. Also, for plans with less than $1 million in assets, a group annuity contract may yet be the most cost effective because of minimum fees charged by service providers using non-insurance products. Either way, it is very important for you as a participant to know how your plan's variable annuity contract works, if one has been adopted by your employer, and what specific charges you are paying. Be aware, however, that according to a 401(k) plan survey conducted by the U.S. Government Accountability Office ("GAO") between October 2010 and 2012[11], 17% of employers surveyed did not know if their plans had group variable annuity contracts, highlighting once again the need for participants to ferret out how their plans are structured.

5. Hidden Fees

Curiously, a mutual fund expense ratio is not required to include the trading expenses – commissions and differences between "bid" and "ask" prices - incurred by the fund in buying and selling securities. Instead, these expenses are deducted by a fund before determining the investment return and the expense ratio. In this way, these expenses are hidden from investor view. You would assume that if they are not disclosed, they must be minimal. That couldn't be further from the truth.

A 2004 study found that among 11,806 equity mutual funds then tracked by Morningstar a whopping 44% of the real cost of owning mutual funds was hidden, amounting to some $17.3 billion dollars.[12]

On a relative basis, trading expenses can vary between 0.65% for the average equity mutual fund, 0.30% for very large mutual funds, and as much as 3.58% for the highest turnover mutual fund.[13] Turnover is expressed as a ratio representing the number of times that a fund portfolio is replaced in a given year, and, since you're not told how much a fund incurs for trading expenses, knowing a fund's turnover ratio is the only way to determine if a fund incurs high trading costs: the more that securities are traded, the higher the trading costs. At the end of the day, there's not much you can do about this and portfolio turnover is a weak indicator of whether a fund is a prudent choice. However, when investors express mistrust about "Wall Street", a lack of transparency, such as with trading costs, is one of the issues they point to, and you need to be aware of it.

6. Summary

We learned in chapter 1 that investment fees make up the majority of the expense of your participation in a 401(k) plan. However, in this chapter, we have learned that what you are charged as investment fees may include fees for services that are totally unrelated to the management of your investments and that these charges are an indirect cost of participating in your 401(k) plan.

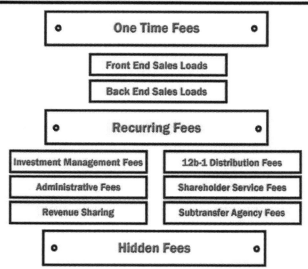

Components of Mutual Fund Fees

Some would say that if a fund has reasonable returns after expenses, why care about the expenses? That is a fair comment. However, if the expenses you're paying are more than reasonable, there is a problem because they are unnecessarily and imprudently eating away at your returns and retirement income prospects. The purpose of this chapter is to have helped you become a more educated investor and to teach you that, in addition to evaluating a fund's investment performance, you have to pay attention to factors such as a fund's share class, potential sales charges, expense ratio, the level of revenue sharing and, lastly, portfolio turnover.

When all is said and done, what should you be paying in administration and investment expenses?

In the earlier chapter, we quoted statistics from the 401(k) Averages Book, 15th Edition. As a recap, for plans with 10 participants and $500,000 in assets, the average bundled cost of administration and investment fees was $953 per year. This represents 1.91% of assets, whereas for a plan with 2,000 participants and $20 million in assets, the average bundled cost per year was $127, and this represents 1.27% of assets.

Number of Participants	Total Plan Assets	Average Per Participant Cost	Cost as Percentage of Assets
10	$500,000	$953	1.91%
2,000	$20,000,000	$127	1.27%

In their 2013 study of defined contribution/401(k) plan fees[14], Deloitte found that what they call the average "All-In" Fee, which includes administration and investment costs, ranges from 1.17% for plans with $1 million but less than $10 million in assets, to 0.89% for plans with $10 million but less than $20 million in assets.

So you can see that there is some variation in these statistics, but you can use them as a guide to test how your plan compares.

7. Your employer's responsibilities

When a business starts a 401(k) plan, it is faced with the need to engage one or more service providers to handle a number of tasks, which include:

- Setting up the plan and enrolling participants;

- Keeping track of participants' accounts, contributions, investment directions, loans, distributions and the like;

- Preparing plan documents, getting IRS approval and handling government reporting, and participant disclosures;

- Selecting and overseeing the plan's investment fund menu;

- Determining if and how revenue sharing should be used; and

- Providing participants with investment education.

401(k) plans are subject to government regulation: the Employee Retirement Income Security Act of 1974 (ERISA), overseen by the DOL, and the Internal Revenue Code, overseen by the IRS. As mentioned in the Introduction, under ERISA, employers, and those appointed by them with authority over the management and/or administration of the plan or its assets

(whom we call "fiduciaries"), are subject to a number of responsibilities to ensure that the plan is operated prudently, in the best interests of the participants and for their exclusive benefit. As a consequence, fiduciaries have to exercise due care when selecting service providers and making other decisions.

Ideally, fiduciaries will select service providers as a result of a competitive bidding process. That involves issuing a Request for Proposal (RFP) to several different providers who then respond with a description of their services and fees so that the fiduciaries can select the one that offers the services most suited to the needs of the plan at a reasonable cost. In practice, many employers do not use competitive bidding but nonetheless they must be able to demonstrate that they made a prudent decision in selecting service providers and that service providers charge a reasonable fee and provide services that are suited to the needs of the plan. As we saw in the first chapter, this does not mean that the cheapest provider must be selected, as many people think. If a particular service provider is found to offer better quality services but charges more, selection of that provider may still meet the test of prudence.

When selecting service providers, among the decisions that an employer must make, the following are key:

- What are the reasonable plan administration costs per participant?

- Will the employer pay for the plan's administration costs out of its own pocket or out of plan assets?

- If the costs of administration are to be paid out of plan assets, how will that be done? By a direct charge to each participant's account? Or, by revenue sharing?

- If revenue sharing is to be used, what amount for this purpose is built into the expense ratio of selected mutual fund or non-mutual fund investments?

- Is the expense ratio reasonable for each investment fund selected?

- What is a fair method to allocate revenue sharing among participants

Some plan providers offer a "bundled" program where they are the source of the investment funds and recordkeeping and administration services. This happens, for example, with insurance companies who offer variable annuity contracts. It has been known for such providers to suggest to employers that they don't have to worry about administration costs because neither the employer nor plan participants will get billed for them. In other words, the provider is going to take care of the plan administration costs out of the funds' expense ratios through revenue sharing. It is such an approach, of course, that gives rise to the notion that 401(k) plans are free, but, as we now know, that is untrue.

One of the problems with the example just given is that the employer does not know what the cost of administration is and, therefore, the employer can't make a determination whether that cost is "reasonable", as required by ERISA. Furthermore, you as a participant may not be properly informed of what is charged to your account for plan administration. While this information is required to be disclosed to you, some disclosures don't give you exact information but refer you to another document in which the information may be buried.

The example given also highlights that, irrespective of payment arrangements, the employer must know what the administration cost is in order to test its reasonableness. However, the employer also needs this information in order to determine whether revenue sharing is sufficient to cover that cost and, if not, how will the excess be paid? Conversely, the employer needs to know whether revenue sharing payments will exceed the cost of administration, in which case, the excess must be used for the benefit of the plan participants, not for the benefit of the employer or the service providers.

To put this issue in perspective, consider the 401(k) survey findings of the April 2012 GAO Report previously referred to[15], where 9% of employers reported that they did not know if 401(k) recordkeeping and administrative fees were paid and 7% said that such fees were waived! In either case, the likelihood is that, unbeknownst to the employer, recordkeeping and administrative fees were being passed on to the participants through revenue sharing. It should be noted that these findings preceded the July 2012 introduction of DOL regulation requiring greater fee transparency. So, things may have changed, but there is little evidence of that yet and participants are burdened with the need to ferret things out.

As part of the evaluation of revenue sharing, the employer must also approve the share class of selected mutual funds. As we have seen, that selection influences the level of expense ratio and revenue sharing that the plan will experience. Of course, if the employer has elected to pay the plan administration costs, it would be imprudent to select a share class that includes revenue sharing because, you, as a participant, would then be paying for the same services that the employer is paying for and someone else would be receiving a windfall, unless the revenue sharing would be credited back to the plan.

However, even if the employer has elected to use revenue sharing, selecting a share class with revenue sharing when another share class is available without revenue sharing will be regarded as imprudent, if revenue sharing was not a factor that was considered when selecting that fund. That may seem odd but that's what was decided in Tibble v. Edison, a case that went before the U.S. Supreme Court.

As we have also seen, employers who adopt revenue sharing must make a prudent choice as to how revenue sharing is implemented because, if the funds selected have varying levels of revenue sharing and some funds have no revenue sharing, participants will bear plan costs disproportionately and some participants may pay nothing!

An employer's obligation does not end with selection decisions.

Once the initial selection of service providers and investment funds has been made, fiduciaries have an ongoing obligation to periodically monitor service providers and investment funds to ensure that they remain prudent choices. What is a reasonable interval for monitoring depends on a number of factors, including the size of the plan and the complexity of the investments. But it is fair to say that the employer and plan fiduciaries should evaluate every year whether the plan is meeting objectives, and that they should take appropriate action if not.

8. Questions to ask your employer

Armed with what you have learned in this chapter, here are some questions to ask your employer if you don't have access to the information you need to understand and monitor the investment expenses which you bear. Note that the first 3 questions are similar to the first 3 questions suggested in Chapter 1. They are repeated because these questions underscore the importance of an employer's fiduciary responsibilities in relation to controlling plan expenses.

1. How were our service providers selected?
2. Did you use an RFP?
3. If no RFP, how did you evaluate the reasonableness of services and fees?
4. How am I charged for administration costs?
5. Am I paying for administration costs through revenue sharing?
6. How much is the revenue sharing?
7. Which mutual fund share classes have the plan purchased?
8. What is the ticker symbol for each of our funds? (You can use this to verify the share class.)
9. Were cheaper share classes available when funds were selected?
10. If a more expensive share class was selected, why?

11. If the plan offers ETFs, what trading costs do I incur when I select those investments or redeem them in favor of other funds?
12. If the plan uses a group variable annuity:
    a) What are the underlying mutual funds?
    b) What mutual fund share class is being purchased by the insurance company?
    c) What insurance company fees am I paying and why?
13. What is being done to equalize fees among participants?
14. Why are we paying a sales charge (only if applicable)?
15. To whom were sales charges paid and what services did they provide (only if applicable)?
16. What fee benchmarking does the plan conduct?
17. Has fee benchmarking led to any changes?
18. Have our fund share classes been evaluated in light of fiduciary breach litigation and fund companies' efforts to make share classes more fiduciary appropriate?

---

[6] *Investment Company Institute. 2015. 2015 Investment Company Fact Book: A Review of Trends and Activity in the Investment Company Industry. Washington, DC: Investment Company Institute. Available at* http://www.icifactbook.org

[7] *Investment Company Institute. ICI Research Perspective, July 2014, volume 20, NO.3*

[8] *Investment Company Institute. 2015. 2015 Investment Company Fact Book: A Review of Trends and Activity in the Investment Company Industry. Washington, DC: Investment Company Institute.*

[9] *Share Class Offerings Shift With Fiduciary Focus,* Planadviser, August 31, 2015: http://www.planadviser.com/Share-Class-Offerings-Shift-With-Fiduciary-Focus/

[10] http://www.bloomberg.com/news/articles/2014-10-08/an-investor-s-guide-to-fees-and-expenses-2014

[11] GAO, April 2012, *401(K) Plans, Increased Educational Outreach and Broader Oversight May Help Reduce Plan Fees.*

[12] *Karceski, Jason; Miles Livingston; and Edward S. O'Neal. Portfolio Transactions Cost at U.S. Equity Mutual Funds. 2004*

[13] *Karceski, Jason; Miles Livingston; and Edward S. O'Neal. Portfolio Transactions Cost at U.S. Equity Mutual Funds. 2004*

[14] *Inside the Structure of Defined Contribution/401(K) plan Fee, 2013.* Deloitte Consulting LLP

[15] GAO, April 2012 *401(K) Plans, Increased Educational Outreach and Broader Oversight May Help Reduce Plan Fees.*

Chapter 3: Fund Selection

What you will learn:

1. **Your decisions upon enrollment**
2. **The decisions for which your employer is responsible when creating the fund menu**
3. **Passive v. Active investment management**
4. **The employer's selection of fund categories**
5. **The employer's selection of specific funds**
6. **Employer relief from liability for participant investment losses**
7. **Questions to ask your employer**

1. Your decisions upon enrollment

When you first enroll in a 401(k) plan, you are confronted with a number of important decisions:

1. What percentage of your compensation to contribute to the plan on a pre-tax basis – Yes, what you contribute is deducted before your compensation is taxed, which is why there are limits on what you may defer;

2. What investment funds to select from the plan's fund menu;

3. How contributions should be allocated among the funds you selected; and

4. Who to name as beneficiary in the event that you should die while still participating in the plan.

The enrollment material will guide you on these matters and Part II of this guide will help you establish sound strategies. Because it is important for people to start saving for retirement as soon as they start working, your plan may allow your employer to automatically enroll you in the plan at a given contribution rate. You are then free to opt out, or to alter your contribution rate if you decide to stay in the plan. Based on your automatic enrollment, related plan provisions will result in automatic investment of your contributions in one of the plan's investment funds specifically selected by the employer to receive so called "default" contributions. Of course, if these provisions apply to your plan, you will have the right to change the investment selection.

Later in this guide (see Chapter 10), you will read about sound strategies that can assist you in deciding the right amount to contribute, the way in which to select funds and the appropriate allocation of your contributions between them. In this part of the guide, we will look at how employers select funds and why it's important for you to understand this.

As you now know, employers have a fiduciary responsibility to act with due care and in your best interests when they make a decision about the management of your plan and the investments. These responsibilities affect the way in which employers select and manage the funds available in a plan, but it is important for you to know at the outset that the responsibility for how much you contribute to your plan and how you allocate your contributions among available funds rests entirely with you.

2. The decisions for which your employer is responsible when creating the fund menu

So, getting back to the employer's responsibilities in selecting funds, there are a number of preliminary decisions that the employer has to make, which are usually reflected in a document which the employer adopts and is known as an Investment Policy Statement (IPS). This is the employer's road map or business plan for guiding the employer, or its investment committee, if it has appointed one, in how to select, monitor, and replace funds. The employer's decisions include:

1. Whether to select "passive" or "active" investment management;
2. Which fund categories should be reflected in the fund menu;
3. How specific funds should be selected for inclusion in the plan's fund menu;
4. Whether, as allowed by ERISA, the plan will claim relief from liability for investment losses resulting from individual participant investment decisions.

3. Passive v. Active Investment Management

The employer's selection process begins with deciding whether the plan should use passively managed funds or actively managed funds. Passively managed funds generally take the form of "index funds" where the manager is seeking to replicate the performance of a particular market index, such as the S&P 500 or the Russell 2000, whereas actively managed funds will invest in a narrower basket of securities chosen as part of the manager's strategy to outperform a selected index.

By way of explanation, a market index combines the total value of investments within a market segment, expressed as a single value that can be tracked to measure changes over time. The Dow Jones Industrial Average is, perhaps, the best recognized market index, or the S&P 500 or the Russell 2000. Passively managed Index funds, as we said, are intended to replicate a particular index.

So, how does the employer decide? The debate over the strengths and weaknesses of active v. passive investment has raged for a long time and there are respected authorities on both sides, but there is an important distinction that an employer should examine.

No active manager can continuously "beat the market", meaning the index chosen by a manager as a benchmark for measuring a fund's investment performance. Most managers will tell you that it is their goal to achieve higher investment returns than their benchmark index "over a market cycle". This means that, in order to get the benefit of their particular investment strategy, you have to remain invested in the fund for a long period of time, measured as a "market cycle".

Unsurprisingly, this is not well defined, but generally represents a period of time during which particular market conditions favor the manager's investment strategy, such as low oil prices, or high interest rates. The problem is that, as investors, we don't necessarily know how to monitor market cycles and we simply count on active managers to exploit anomalies in the market by placing winning bets on investment outcomes through the selection of particular securities. In any event, investing in actively managed funds is intended to be a long term strategy, meaning that we're not meant to switch in and out of such funds but "stay the course" to allow sufficient time for the manager's strategy to work.

This guide is not a work on behavioral finance, but there is evidence to suggest that many 401(k) participants do not hold the course but switch out of fund choices prematurely, usually when the fund share price is depressed. This, of course, defeats the purpose of investing in actively managed funds. Considering this behavioral tendency, the question is whether it is prudent for an employer to offer actively managed funds in the plan's fund menu?

The answer, in part, relies on the role of investment diversification. One of the employer's fiduciary responsibilities is to "diversify" the assets of the plan. To "diversify" assets means to mix a wide variety of investments within a portfolio. The purpose is to spread the risk and opportunity for return among a mix of investments so that on average you achieve a higher return than if you simply invested in a single investment within the portfolio. There are additional ways to increase diversification, of course, such as by selecting investments from different fund categories, for example, stocks and bonds and, as we have said, selecting different fund categories is one of the decisions an employer must make.

While some suggest that the duty to diversify compels an employer to offer only index funds because such funds offer the broadest opportunity for diversification, it is well accepted by the investment community that mutual funds which are actively managed offer sufficient intrinsic diversification through the purchase of securities of multiple issuers, that such funds satisfy an employer's obligation regarding investment diversification, even though the underlying securities don't replicate the entire market represented by the chosen index.

However, an employer is expected to evaluate these matters when selecting funds and if the employer is satisfied that, over time, offering funds with active management will lead to better investment outcomes for participants, the decision to select actively managed funds will be considered to be prudent.

Of course, many plans cater to both investment philosophies by offering both index funds and actively managed funds. In addition, many employers engage service providers to educate participants on investment management, and this education, if properly delivered, will address the role of passive versus active management and the need to take a long term view when participants select funds from the plan's investment menu. As a participant, you should consider these matters when you make your own fund selections.

4. The Employer's Fund Category Selection

Having made decisions about the use of passive and/or actively managed funds, the employer must decide the fund categories from which funds will be selected. Fund categories are generally comprised of equity and fixed income funds but can be subdivided, for example, into:

Large cap growth equities

Large cap value equities

Midcap equities

Small cap equities

Foreign equities

Short term fixed income

Intermediate fixed income

Long term fixed income, both government and corporate, domestic or foreign

In addition, there are asset allocation fund categories such as a balanced fund category, in which both equity and income investments are included; a target date fund category, in which the allocation between equities and bonds is managed to reduce risk as you get closer to retirement; and a lifestyle fund category, in which portfolios are established to meet different risk profiles, such as conservative, moderate and aggressive.

Generally, an employer will take advice on these matters and select categories that permit broad diversification.

5. The Employer's Specific Fund Selection

Then, having selected fund categories, the employer will select particular funds from each such category. To guide this selection, the employer should first establish fund selection criteria, usually with professional investment advice. The resulting criteria will be recorded in the IPS.

Typically, fund selection criteria will focus on the following:

1. Acceptable parameters for Investment performance relative to peers (i.e. comparable funds) and benchmarks – The employer must decide how high a fund needs to be in the pack in terms of investment performance.

2. Acceptable parameters for consistency of style – The manager shouldn't stray too much from the investment style that a fund advertises, e.g. a stock fund seeking dividend income should not have a heavy weighting towards growth stocks, which typically don't yield a lot of dividend income.

3. Minimum permitted Investment Manager Team tenure – The manager should have held that job for a minimum period, e.g. 3 or 5 years, so that the manager can demonstrate a reasonable track record.

4. Minimum permitted assets under management for liquidity – The employer should set a minimum limit on the assets in a fund to ensure that the fund has enough assets to meet general redemption demand without devaluing the fund.

5.   Absence of regulatory issues or litigation – You don't want a fund which has issues that interfere with money management.

6.   Timeliness and accuracy of investment reporting according to Global Investment Performance Standards – The fund must be able to provide the employer with timely investment reports that meet industry standards.

7.   Adequate back office function – The fund should have sufficient resources for research, trading, accounting, compliance and customer service.

8.   Fair and reasonable investment costs – Investment fees must be reasonable and not among the highest for comparable funds.

9.   Acceptable mutual fund share classes based on whether or not revenue sharing is used to pay plan expenses – Select only the lowest cost share class for the services actually required, which need not be the cheapest class. (See earlier discussion).

Remember, having selected funds, the employer must also periodically monitor the funds to ensure that they still conform to the selection criteria or to some other prudently determined criteria.

6. Employer Relief from Liability for Participant Investment Losses

We mentioned earlier that, as a participant, you are solely responsible for the plan fund choices you make and for how you allocate contributions among them. It follows that the employer is not responsible for any losses you incur as a result of your decisions. However, in order for an employer to secure relief from such losses, the employer has certain obligations towards you.

- First, you must be given the opportunity to control your investments. This is generally satisfied by your having access to your account so that you can give investment direction on a daily basis and by your receiving information necessary for you to make informed

  investment decisions. This information is governed by DOL regulation[16] and is commonly made available with your enrollment material, but some information is made available only upon request. Your enrollment materials should explain this. It is important to note that if your employer has failed to provide this information, your employer will likely be guilty of a fiduciary breach. Because of the importance of this obligation, your employer will have likely delegated this function to your plan's recordkeeper or third party administrator.

- Secondly, you must be permitted to choose from a

  "broad range of investment alternatives" that allow you to; (a) materially affect the potential return and the degree of risk in your portfolio (i.e. meet different risk v. return objectives); and (b) diversify the investments to minimize the risk of large losses.

- Thirdly, the employer must notify you in the Summary Plan Description, a document you receive at enrollment, of its intention to claim relief from liability for investment losses resulting from your investment directions.

The second requirement discussed above brings us back to the issue of diversification and the meaning of a "broad range of investment alternatives". The DOL regulation references a minimum of three alternatives. However, investment professionals generally suggest a minimum of six funds such as:

U.S large cap growth equity fund

U.S large cap value equity fund

U.S. small cap equity fund

International equity fund

Bond fund

Stable value fund or insurance company general account fund

These may be supplemented by a balanced fund, a series of lifestyle funds or by target date funds.

7. Questions to Ask Your Employer

As we have said elsewhere, your ability to use your 401(k) plan to provide a secure retirement income is impacted by decisions made by your employer. We have previously seen that your employer's decisions regarding plan fees and how they are to be paid have a significant impact on your ability to save. In this chapter, we have seen how your employer's decisions regarding fund selection impact your opportunities to invest your savings, which is why you need to know the process your employer is expected to follow.

As a participant, you are entitled to assume that each fund offered through your plan has been prudently selected and monitored and is suitable for inclusion in the portfolio you create.

However, if after reading this chapter, you have concerns about your fund menu, there is no reason why you cannot raise them with your employer. The following is a sample of questions you could raise if the circumstances warranted.

1. Would you please provide a copy of the plan's Investment Policy Statement?

Bear in mind that ERISA specifies which documents an employer is bound to supply you. Such documents are referred to as "plan documents". The IPS is not among them, but an employer is certainly free to provide participants with a copy and law suits have challenged an employer's refusal to disclose the IPS. In most cases, the challenge has been unsuccessful, but in others the courts have favored disclosure at least of parts that can help participants understand their rights or benefits. Accordingly, in our view, there is nothing inappropriate in making such a request and an employer which is meeting its fiduciary responsibilities has nothing to fear from disclosure. Transparency is key to building participants' trust in the merits of their plan and a refusal to disclose the IPS, while the request may be uncommon, certainly impinges on that trust. If an employer declines to provide a copy, the declination prompts other questions:

a) Is there an IPS in place?

b) Has an investment committee been appointed? If so, who are the members?

c) How did the employer/investment committee decide which fund categories to include in the investment menu?

d) How did the employer/investment committee decide which specific funds to include in the investment menu? What selection criteria were applied?

e) What did the employer/investment committee consider when deciding to use only actively managed funds? (Obviously, you would not ask the question if the investment menu includes index funds.)

Roger Levy and Peter Roland

f) How often does the employer/investment committee monitor and evaluate the funds they selected?

g) Does the employer/investment committee use an independent investment advisor to assist with fund selection, monitoring and replacement?

h) Who pays for the independent investment advisor?

i) If participants pay for the independent investment advisor, how much are we paying?

j) Is the independent investment advisor's fee included in the costs shown in my quarterly investment statement? If not, where is it reported?

k) Has the employer delivered all of the information required of the employer for me to make an informed investment decision? A list of required disclosures can be found at: www.dol.gov/ebsa

[16] 29 C.F.R. § 2550.404a-5

Chapter 4: Allocation Funds, QDIAs, and Target Date Funds

What you will learn:

1. What are "allocation" funds
2. What is a Qualified Default Investment Alternative (QDIA)
3. Target Date Fund (TDF) elements
4. TDF Selection Criteria
5. What else you need to know about TDFs
6. TDF Lessons Learned
7. Auto Re-enrollment
8. TDF fees
9. Questions to ask your employer

Introduction

There are two key factors which you control as a 401(k) plan participant that will ultimately dictate how much retirement income your 401(k) plan can generate for you. The first is how much you contribute to your account over time, and the second is how well you manage the investments. Of course, the general economy, inflation, interest rates, and whether you receive an employer matching contribution or not all impact the investment outcome, but you have no control over these matters.

We mentioned earlier that many plan participants have a poor track record of making sound investment choices when it comes to their plan investments. Some participants are too conservative, some take on too much risk, and some switch between investments at inopportune times, all of which can damage retirement income prospects.

1. Allocation Funds

Over time, the 401(k) industry and employers have sought ways to help participants avoid these pitfalls and to improve their retirement income prospects. This has led to the introduction of investment funds that allow for the transfer of the decision making process from participants to investment professionals who can better manage the allocation of investments between investment classes or categories, which is recognized among investment professionals as the principal driver of investment returns. Such funds include:

a) **Balanced Funds**, where the manager combines stocks and bonds in a single portfolio, either favoring stocks (moderate risk) or bonds (conservative risk) with little variation in that allocation over time;

b) **Lifestyle Funds or Target Risk Funds**, which invest in a mix of stocks and bonds using conservative, moderate or aggressive growth strategies, and allow participants to align their risk and return appetites to a corresponding fund;

c) **Lifecycle or Target Date Funds**, which pursue a long-term investment strategy, using a mix of stocks and bonds, that is adjusted over time to become more conservative as a participant draws towards retirement or a date beyond;

d) **Managed Accounts**, where portfolios are created based on a participant's age or retirement date but use only the fund choices otherwise available under the plan;

e) **Asset Allocation Models**, where portfolios are created using the fund choices available under the plan to meet conservative, moderate or aggressive risk and return objectives. You often find these in plans where the employer has hired an investment adviser to help with fund selection and the adviser provides asset allocation models as one of its services.

The availability of these funds represents a significant improvement in 401(k) plan investment options and there has been a shift towards the use of these alternatives, particularly target date funds, which have become popular largely due to government regulation.

Back in 1998, as a response to low participation rates in 401(k) plans, the IRS issued a ruling to permit newly eligible employees to be automatically enrolled. Following automatic enrollment, unless participants then made an investment election, employers would deposit participant contributions in the plan investment fund which represented the greatest perceived safety, usually a money market fund, generally referred to as a "default" alternative because it was selected by the employers.

They did so with the expectation that participants would migrate their investments into other funds that would allow diversification and growth. Many participants did not take advantage of these opportunities and left the money where it lay, in cash, leading to another concern that money market funds were not suitable as a permanent default investment choice, because they lacked any growth potential. However, employers were unwilling to make "automatic" changes to the default selection because of the risk of fiduciary liability.

2. Qualified Default Investment Alternative ("QDIA")

In 2006, the Pension Protection Act was passed and provided employers with relief from fiduciary responsibility for participant losses resulting from an employer's selection of the investment fund to which participant contributions would be directed as a result of a participant's failure to give investment direction, for example, as a result of automatic enrollment.

However, to obtain this relief, the investment fund so selected had to meet certain criteria as a Qualified Default Investment Alternative, or "QDIA" as you will see it called in your plan materials.

In order for an investment fund to meet the requirements of a QDIA, an employer must select from one of the following:

1. A balanced fund as described above in paragraph 1. a);
2. A managed account described above in paragraph 1. d);
3. A target date or lifecycle fund as described above in paragraph 1. c).

Today, of the available QDIA choices, the target date fund category (TDF) is by far and away the most popular among employers.

The popularity of TDF's is reflected in industry statistics.

According to the Investment Company Institute, target date mutual funds received $53 billion in new cash flows during 2013, compared to $22 billion in 2005 and $4 billion in 2002.[17] As of June 2014, the Investment Company Institute found that mutual fund TDF's held approximately $678 billion in assets, and this does not include assets held by TDFs operated as collective investment trusts.

According to Ron Surz, an expert on target date funds, there are some 20 million participants owning TDF assets across 100,000 401(k) plans and he expects TDF assets to reach $4 trillion by 2020.[18] This is unsurprising based on an August 2015 report by the Government Accountability Office (GAO), which found that up to 72% of employers are selecting TDFs as the QDIA for their defined contribution plans.[19]

So, chances are that your plan will have a QDIA and it will likely be in the form of a series of TDFs selected by your employer to reflect the age or prospective retirement date of the participant population. For example, for an individual aged 31 years old in 2016, the TDF selected as appropriate could be the XYZ Target Date Fund 2050, indicating an anticipated retirement at age 65 in 2050. But, for a 46 year old in 2016, the most likely choice would be the XYZ Target Date Fund 2035.

Note that, in terms of 401(k) fund offerings, the availability of TDFs in no way invalidates the suitability of the other types of allocation funds discussed in paragraph 1 above, i.e. Lifestyle funds or Asset Allocation Models. However, neither of these fund types qualifies as a QDIA.

3. Target Date Fund Elements

We stress throughout this guide the importance of your employer's fiduciary responsibility when making decisions regarding the management of your 401(k) plan and its investments. When it comes to investment fund selection, employers are expected to investigate and evaluate their prospective fund choices and reach a prudent decision. This applies equally to the selection of a QDIA. Of course, once selected, the QDIA is available to all participants, not just to those who become enrolled automatically or otherwise fail to give investment directions. However, the fact that a fund was selected for this purpose may represent to participants an implicit endorsement by the employer of the general suitability of the selected QDIA, thereby increasing the need for close scrutiny.

So let's take a more detailed look at TDFs.

In essence, a TDF is a managed portfolio holding a mix of stocks, bonds and other investments that increase diversification (such as hedge funds, private equity funds and even commodities) where the mix changes automatically over time as the participant ages. Initially, the mix, or "asset allocation", as investment professionals call it, favors stocks because stocks are expected to yield higher returns than bonds, and the risks associated with those returns, which are also higher than in the case of bonds, are more easily absorbed when a participant is young. As the retirement age draws nearer, the asset allocation changes to reduce the risks associated with stocks by switching more money to bonds. The process by which the asset allocation is managed is called the "glide path" and a target date fund's glide path thus becomes one of its most important features.

In some TDFs, the glide path manages the asset allocation up to the date of retirement. These are known as "to" funds, because they manage the asset allocation "to" the point of retirement. In other TDFs, the glide path is managed through the retirement date to a point beyond, say, till projected mortality, at age 90. These TDFs are known as "through" funds. The distinction is important because, at the retirement date, a

"through" fund will likely have a higher exposure to stocks than a "to" fund. The rationale for "through" funds is that they cater to the needs of participants who will remain invested in the plan following retirement. We speak more about glide paths in section 5 of this chapter.

Generally, TDFs are established as a "fund of funds", where the investment firm which manages the TDF assembles a group of other funds (we refer to these funds as "sub funds"), each with its own manager, to invest in the stock component, the bond component and any other asset class component that makes up the TDF's portfolio. Accordingly, the investment firm managing the TDF plays a key role and is responsible for:

1. Determining whether the fund will be a "to" or "through" fund;

2. Establishing the glide path;

3. Determining whether asset allocation will be "strategic", i.e. the glide path is set and will be followed without deviation, or "tactical", where the allocation will be impacted over time by shifts in the market;

4. Determining the use of passive or active management;

5. Establishing asset class selection (Stocks, bonds, other); and

6. Determining whether to use their own internal sub funds, known as "proprietary" funds, or sub funds managed by nonaffiliated external managers, known as "non-proprietary" funds.

The decisions made by a TDF manager, in regard to these matters, result in considerable differences between TDFs and how they perform. Accordingly, employers must investigate and evaluate these differences before making a selection. The use of proprietary sub funds bears particular scrutiny, although the majority of TDF managers use them. The rationale for non-proprietary funds is that, if the objective is to populate a TDF with sub funds that represent "best in class" opportunities for each asset class selected, the use of proprietary funds could be limiting in that regard. Put another way, can you find the best sub fund line up within a single fund family?

4. TDF Selection Criteria

With that understanding, let's look at the particular duties that an employer has in regard to TDFs.

We mentioned in Chapter 3, when discussing fund selection, that your employer should establish an investment policy statement (IPS) which should include, among other things, criteria for the selection of the specific funds to be included in the plan's fund menu. This is to ensure that the employer has a consistently applied process for picking one fund over another.

In the case of TDFs, their complexity calls for additional vigilance, as we have seen. Accordingly, the employer should establish selection criteria specific to this complexity. Such criteria should address:

1. Selection of "to" or "through" fund – The employer must establish which arrangement is best suited to the participant population;

2. Selection of glide path – the role of equities and the pace of change in allocation – The employer must decide whether to pick a glide path directed towards preservation of capital (i.e. conservative), generally a "to" fund, or towards meeting longevity and inflation protection needs (aggressive), generally a "through" fund;

3. The application of strategic or tactical allocation – The employer must ascertain whether to select TDFs where the manager will adjust the glide path to meet changing market conditions or TDFs where the manager adheres to the chosen glide path allocation, irrespective of market conditions, and periodically rebalances the portfolio to conform to that allocation, if market conditions have caused a change;

4. Use of passive/active management – The employer must determine which investment philosophy it favors in a TDF environment, or whether to seek a TDF which incorporates both. (See earlier discussion on passive/active management in Chapter 3);

5. Fund structure – Generally, TDFs may be established as a mutual fund or as a collective trust (see earlier discussion). The employer must decide which is suitable given cost and the size of the plan;

6. The TDF manager's process for selecting and replacing sub fund managers – The employer must approve the process in place;

7. The range of permitted fees and expenses of a TDF and sub funds – The employer must determine what fees participants should expect to pay, taking into account fees of the TDF manager and managers of sub funds. Such fees should be reasonable and not among the highest;

8. Selection of proprietary versus nonproprietary sub funds or of a mix – The employer should determine whether the plan will offer proprietary TDFs operated by a single family of funds or whether to select a provider who offers non-proprietary sub funds representing "best in class" opportunities. In evaluating TDFs with non-proprietary sub funds, the employer should determine whether that strategy increases fees and improves performance in contrast to TDFs using proprietary sub funds;

9. The proposed TDF series should be suitable based on current and historic participant demographics and/or average risk tolerance assessment – The employer should undertake some assessment of the demographics, such as participation levels, contribution rates, loan activity and level of cash-outs at retirement. Or, the employer might test participants' risk tolerance levels. (Note that the scrutiny is needed because the universe of TDFs offers significant variations in risk profile and investment performance.); and

10. The TDF manager should offer a quality participant communications strategy and quality educational material – The employer should require these features, given the complexity of TDFs and the need for participants to be well informed.

Target Date Funds (TDF) Criteria

Use of "To" or "Through" Fund	Manager's Process for Selecting and Replacing Sub Fund Managers
Glide Path Selection	Range of Permitted Fees and Expenses
Application of Strategic/Tactical Allocation	Proprietary/Non-Proprietary Sub Funds
Use of Passive/Active Management	Suitability Based on Participant Demographics
Fund Structure	Communications Strategy and Education

Having established selection criteria, the employer will then conduct a search, often with the help of an investment adviser, to identify fund management companies that offer TDFs which meet the established criteria, just as the employer must do when selecting other funds. The employer will then perform due diligence, meaning that the employer will examine funds (preferably using a RFP process to test their conformity with the selection criteria. The employer will then narrow the choice to a few finalists who would then be subjected to an interview. Following interviews, the employer will make its selection.

Since the selection of funds has a significant impact on how participants allocate their account balances over time, employers can't simply make an initial selection and file away the paperwork. There is an obligation to periodically take a look at what was selected and why, to ensure that the initial decisions remain prudent. Accordingly, employers must establish monitoring criteria. In all likelihood they will be similar to the selection criteria.

5. What Else You Need to Know About TDFs

Thus far, we have talked about how TDFs evolved, how important they are as a QDIA, how they offer automatic management of your investment portfolio and change the risk level over time. We have also talked about the complexity of TDFs and your employer's fiduciary responsibilities in selecting TDFs and monitoring them on a periodic basis. The discussion should provide a valuable reference point as you look at the TDFs available under your plan. **But we can't leave the topic of TDFs without further discussion of TDF glide paths and their differences.**

As we have explained, the objective of a TDF's glide path is to manage investment risk by changing the balance between stock and bond investments over time.

Much is dictated by whether the TDF is a "to" or a "through" fund.

A "to" fund will generally have the objective of helping participants meet their accumulation goals at retirement and will have a glide path that becomes more conservative around the retirement date, on the assumption that participants will then leave the plan and/or begin withdrawing from the account. Such a fund may have an allocation toward stocks of 35% to 50% around the target date.

A "through" fund will generally have the objective of maximizing savings through retirement and will have a more aggressive posture towards stocks around the retirement date, because participants are expected to remain invested for a number of years following retirement, say 5 – 30 years, and will want protection from longevity risk (outliving your money) and inflation risk (consumer price increases). Such a fund may have an allocation in stocks of 55% - 75% around the target date.

But these are rules of thumb and variations in glide path structure can be found among fund families irrespective of whether a fund is designated "to" or "through".

Employers who select "through" funds for their participants are impliedly encouraging participants to remain invested in their TDF beyond retirement so that they can better protect themselves from longevity risk and inflation risk. Supporting this posture, experts point to a number of considerations.

- First, if you are looking to your 401(k) plan as your sole source of retirement income, bear in mind that government regulation limits what you may contribute. Between 2009 and 2015, the contribution limit has gone from $16,500 to $18,000, with catch up limits for those 50 or over, going from $5,500 to $6,000. Investment experts say that, even allowing for employer contributions, these government contribution limits coupled with greater life expectancy make it difficult to provide the replacement income one will need at retirement, generally thought to be 80% of final working compensation, without having the majority of one's investments in stocks at retirement and beyond.

- Secondly, investment experts will tell you that a common rule of thumb that you should substantially reduce your allocation to stocks as you age is an outdated standard because it was developed in an age of higher bond yields than exist today.

Because there are significant differences in glide path construction between "to" and "through" funds, and from one fund family to another, it is very important for you as a participant to know what weighting towards stocks will be created by your TDF's glide path. History teaches us how important that is.

In 2008, when the stock market plunged and heralded in the Great Recession, many 2010 target dates funds, i.e. those designed for participants about to retire in 2010, lost 25% to 35% of their value. The majority of these TDFs had an allocation to stocks of over 50%. One fund, Oppenheimer Transition 2010 A, lost 41.32% while holding 65% of its assets in stocks.[20] Compared to a 37% decline in the Standard & Poor's 500 Index, which of course is comprised exclusively of stocks, one can see that the risk assumed by these 2010 TDFs resulted in significant losses. On the other hand, the average loss of eight 2010 TDFs with stock holdings of less than 40% was 15.4%. One fund, American Independent NestEgg 2010, holding only 26% of its portfolio in stocks, lost 9.11%.

There are experts like Ron Surz who are concerned that the lessons of 2008 have not been learned and that TDF managers still have glide paths that too heavily favor stocks around the retirement date, with potential dire consequences depending on when the next stock market crash occurs. If you are risk averse, you may share that view.

Others argue that many TDF glide paths are designed to be aggressive in order to make up for the failure of participants in general to have saved enough to achieve a secure retirement income. As a result, the argument goes, participants are forced to have an aggressive glide path in terms of stock allocation to ensure that they don't outlive their money.

So, let's look at 401(k) savings rates. According to a 2015 Vanguard report, the average 401(k) participant contribution rate was 6.7% in 2014, down from 7.1% in 2013, and 7.4% in 2012.[21] In contrast, some argue that to achieve retirement readiness, participants should peg their contributions at 15% and that if they begin to do so at age 35 with an allocation in stocks of 89%, that allocation can be safely reduced to 50% by age 65.[22]

It may be that participants gear their contributions towards maximizing their employers match and no more, but the point is that there is a correlation between what you contribute and retirement readiness. Contribution levels, therefore, are part of the demographics that your employer should be considering when selecting a TDF series for your plan.

And herein lies a problem. In a recent survey report[23], under the heading "CAUSE FOR CONCERN", J.P. Morgan found that 83% of employers rated performance as a "very" to an "extremely" important TDF evaluation criterion and that 77% placed fees within the same level of importance. However, only 55% of employers rated glide path structure as "very" to "extremely" important and only 54% ranked participant demographics in that category. Against this background, J.P. Morgan stressed the need for employers, as fiduciaries, to understand "how fundamental differences in the glide path structure and design of TDFs, overlaid with the effects of participant behaviors, can have an impact on the retirement outcomes they hope to help participants achieve." What J.P. Morgan identified as cause for concern for employers are clearly matters of concern for participants.

6. TDF Lessons Learned

So, the lessons from this discussion are that:

a) TDFs offer participants the opportunity of investing in a portfolio that is professionally managed and targeted towards their retirement needs;

b) TDFs are complex investment vehicles;

c) Your employer is making a number of important decisions on your behalf about the TDF series available under your plan;

d) It is crucial for you to understand your employer's decisions and the resulting composition of your TDF, what its objectives are and whether those objectives are suited to your needs. You cannot assume that the last point is so, just because you are invested in a TDF as a result of your employer making a default election on your behalf;

e) You need to make an independent evaluation, paying particular attention to the glide path in terms of your retirement readiness and risk tolerance.

7. Automatic Re-enrollment

A new strategy to steer more participants into TDFs is emerging. This involves auto re-enrollment.

Some employers target participants who have stopped contributing or who have never contributed. In such case, auto re-enrollment allows the employer to impose automatic contributions on these participants and to direct their contributions to the QDIA. Participants must sign a negative election to opt out.

Other employers perform a blanket re-enrollment in the hopes that by steering everyone to the TDF/QDIA they will be providing participants with an age appropriate allocation fund that is more suitable in the employer's view than the individual funds previously selected by the participants. These employers may be relying on participant inertia because participants must sign a new investment direction if they want to retain their existing fund choices.

If your plan has an auto-enrollment feature, the need for scrutinizing your TDF glide path becomes even more crucial because, as we have said, auto-enrollment allows your employer to override your prior investment election and to allocate your entire account to a single TDF, assuming that a TDF is the QDIA, unless you sign a new investment direction to retain your existing fund choices.

In Chapter 3, we mentioned that employers can gain relief from losses in individual participant accounts if participants have the opportunity to control their investments. By using auto re-enrollment to change existing 401(k) investment directions, employers are depriving participants of that control. Some argue that employers still retain their right to fiduciary relief when performing re-enrollment.[24] But this is not clearly supported by DOL regulation and a court would have to agree that a participant's failure to countermand an employer's change in a participant's fund selection represents an exercise of control by that participant.

Knowing that the law is unclear on this point, employers should be taking special care to ensure that their selection of the default investment, typically a TDF, is prudent, because they may well be liable for losses incurred as a result of their interference.

8. TDF Fees

We have discussed fees and expenses earlier, so we know that what you pay for investment fees for TDFs is important because of its impact on investment returns. According to Morningstar, the average TDF expense ratio was 0.84% at the end of 2013[25] but, according to the Investment Company Institute, the average mutual fund expense ratio for TDFs in 2014 was 0.93%.[26] However, fees vary from fund to fund. Vanguard, an industry leader, for example, has an expense ratio of 0.17%, while Fidelity, another industry leader, is lower at 0.16%. Clearly, the trend has been downwards, as with fund fees in general.

9. Questions to Ask Your Employer

The trend in TDF asset growth shows no sign of abating. It warrants your attention.

In this chapter, we have provided a lot of information on TDFs and your employer's role and responsibilities in selecting TDFs and other funds. Since this is not covered in materials provided to participants, the majority of this information will be new to you and will likely prompt a lot of your own questions. In this regard, there is no such thing as a stupid question! There are often stupid answers but this topic is too important to ignore and don't be shy about raising your concerns.

On the other hand, you may find some of the information overwhelming. So, like we have done in other chapters, here are some questions to ask. These should be reviewed in conjunction with the questions in Chapter 2:

1. What criteria were established for the selection of the QDIA?
2. What criteria were established for the selection of TDFs?
3. On what assumptions about participant demographics and risk tolerance was the TDF selection based?
4. What investigation and evaluation was performed before making each selection?
5. Was an investment advisor involved in the selection process?
6. What role did the investment advisor play?
7. Were fund management companies interviewed as part of the selection process?
8. How was the glide path in our TDF series evaluated and determined to be prudent?

9. How was the decision to select either a "to" fund or a "through" fund made and what is its justification?
10. What monitoring is performed to ensure that fund choices remain suitable?
11. How often is monitoring performed?
12. What criteria are applied to monitoring?

13. If auto re-enrollment applies to your plan:
    a) What re-evaluation was made of our plan's QDIA before you performed re-enrollment?
    b) What was the rationale for redirecting my investments to the QDIA? (Only if applicable)
    c) Will you indemnify me for losses resulting from your redirection of my account?

How you use information you receive in response to these questions is up to you of course. But managing your 401(k) account is all about achieving diversification and managing risk according to your own risk tolerance. Hopefully, you will get a good understanding of how and why the TDFs in your plan were selected and you can better determine whether they are suited to your needs unless, of course, you are happy to cede those decisions to your employer.

[17] *Investment Company Institute. October 24, 2014, Frequently Asked Questions About Target Date or Lifecycle Funds.*

[18] *Target Date Funds – Statistics that Matter*, Ron Surz, July 15, 2014. Paladin Registry blog.

[19] 401(K) Plans, Clearer Regulations Could help Plan Sponsors Choose Investments for Participants: Government Accountability Office, August 2015. Note that the report cited three separate surveys by PLANSPONSOR, Callan Investment

Institute and Deloitte, finding that usage of TDFs as the QDIA in 2013 ranged from 59.7% to 72.4%.

[20] *Target-Date Series Research Paper: 2010 Industry Survey*, Morningstar.

[21] 2015 Vanguard Retirement Plan Access™ supplement to *How America Saves*

[22] *Retirement Readiness: 15% salary deferrals are the new 10% for 401(k)s*, Investment News, January 5, 2015. http://www.investmentnews.com/article/20150105/FREE/1501 09978/retirement-readiness-15-salary-deferrals-are-the-new- 10-for-401-k-s

[23] *Aligning goals, improving outcomes*, 2015 Defined Contribution Plan Sponsor Survey Findings, J.P. Morgan Asset Management, at page 16

[24] See *Fiduciary implications: Using re-enrollment to improve target date fund adoption,* A white paper by C. Frederick Reish & Bruce Ashton, Drinker Biddle

[25] *2014 Target Date Series Research Paper*, Morningstar

[26] *Investment Company Institute. 2015. 2015 Investment Company Fact Book: A Review of Trends and Activity in the Investment Company Industry. Washington, DC: Investment Company Institute. Available at www.icifactbook.org.*

Chapter 5: Brokerage Windows

What you will learn:

1. **What is a brokerage window and its features**
2. **What participants need to know about a brokerage window**
3. **Your employers' responsibilities**
4. **Questions to ask your employer**

1. What is a brokerage window and its features?

Many professional employers, CPAs, engineers, lawyers and the like, where the professionals outnumber other employees, find a traditional 401(k) menu of mutual funds too limiting for the personal investment needs of the professional staff. Accordingly, they add another investment feature to the plan consisting of what is known as a "brokerage window". This is nothing more than access to a brokerage account under the umbrella of the plan to permit participants to make investments beyond the fund choices which otherwise make up the plan's fund menu.

Unless the employer designs the brokerage window to limit investments to mutual funds not otherwise available under the plan, sometimes called a "mutual fund only brokerage window", participants are free to invest in stocks, bonds, and other securities.

Brokerage windows are also popular with other employers where management have similar desires to expand their investment opportunities beyond the traditional fund menu.

So what's important for participants to know if your plan has a brokerage window?

2. What participants need to know about a brokerage window

First, your plan investment menu has likely been created with care and skill. If so, you have access to funds that can help you build a diversified portfolio with relative confidence that those funds have been prudently selected. You need to have a good reason, therefore, if you want to stray from this path, and it will take a good degree of investment acumen to achieve a better result.

Secondly, as we have seen, your employer has a fiduciary duty to monitor the funds in your plan and to make changes to the fund lineup if investment performance or other considerations dictate. This added protection is not available for investments you make in a brokerage window, as your employer's oversight responsibilities are thought not to extend to these investments and would thus be limited to the prudent selection of the brokerage firm which provides access to the brokerage window and ongoing oversight of the selected broker. There is an argument to the contrary, and the DOL is toying with regulation that would require employers to perform oversight of investment activity within the broker windows. Unsurprisingly, there appears to be strong opposition from both employers and the broker community and so, if your plan offers a brokerage window, as matters stand, the likelihood is that your employer bears no responsibility for your use of this plan feature.

Further, investing through a brokerage window can be expensive. Transaction fees can be high. Let's say you direct $500 every pay period into a single investment and the cost is $10 per trade. If you are paid bi-weekly, those trading costs amount to $260 per year or 2% of your total investment. Add sale trades and the cost goes up, probably well beyond what you are paying for the funds available under the plan menu.

Even if the employer adopts a mutual fund only brokerage window for the plan, purchasing funds through the window will likely be more costly than investing in the funds available from the plan investment menu. That is because those brokerage window purchases will likely be subject to broker commissions and trading costs, and the share class available to you will typically have a higher expense ratio than those available through the plan investment menu.

Despite the DOL's concerns mentioned above, a recent survey[27] of investment advisory firms, who generally advise large employers on matters like fund selection, found that 56% of these advisors recommend the use of brokerage windows. Of these, 31% recommend a mutual-fund-only brokerage window and 25% recommend a full brokerage window.

3. Employers Responsibilities

As we have indicated, it is the generally held view that an employer's fiduciary responsibilities relating to brokerage windows are less onerous than with respect to other investment features of a 401(k) plan. However, it is certainly true that, if an employer decides that it is in the interests of plan participants to add a brokerage window, the employer must investigate and evaluate the availability of an appropriate brokerage firm who will manage the window, in order for it to be a prudent selection.

In this regard, the employer should look at brokerage charges, the minimum account size required, and other restrictions that may be applied. Indeed, the employer may add its own restrictions, for example, to limit access to highly compensated employees.

However, having made a selection, popular opinion has it that employers do not have the fiduciary responsibility to monitor activity within the brokerage window or, more specifically, the investments purchased by participants through the brokerage window. The justification given is that decisions as to what to buy and sell are made by the participants themselves, not the employer. But this ignores the question of whether offering a brokerage window is prudent in the first place.

In any event, it is our belief that, in general, participants should stay away from brokerage windows. While offering the opportunity for broadening the diversification of assets, that opportunity comes at a high price and potentially with increased risk.

4. Questions to ask your employer

If your plan offers a brokerage window and you either use it or are considering its use, the following questions may be ones to ask your employer:

1. Did you select a brokerage window because of insufficiencies in our plan's fund lineup?
2. If selected for other reasons, please explain?
3. What evaluation was made before selecting a brokerage firm to provide the brokerage window?
4. Has it been verified that the costs associated with using the brokerage window are reasonable and competitive with other providers?
5. Are these costs monitored?

[27] Defined Contribution Consulting Support and Trends Survey, PIMCO 9th Annual Survey Highlights 2015.

Chapter 6: Company Stock Fund, Contributions, and Vesting

What you will learn:

1. **The role of company stock as a 401(k) investment option**
2. **How employer contributions work**
3. **How eligibility and vesting provisions work**
4. **Employer responsibilities**
5. **Questions to ask your employer**

1. The role of company stock as a 401(k) investment option

We have learned previously of the employer's fiduciary duty to construct a 401(k) investment menu that provides you with the opportunity to diversify your investments. However, when ERISA was adopted, it included an exemption from the diversification rule if a plan permits participants to invest in company stock. As a result, publicly traded companies have used company stock as a means of making matching contributions and some plans allow company stock as an investment option for participant contributions. Some privately held companies have also used company stock as a 401(k) investment option.

Company stock funds have enjoyed checkered success. Many publicly traded companies have enjoyed rising stock prices and their employees have shared in that success through 401(k) plan company stock ownership. On the other hand, many companies have suffered serious setbacks and employees who owned company stock through their 401(k) plans shared in the misery.

The most notable fall from grace was Enron, which went bankrupt in 2001 leaving employees holding 60% of their 401(k) assets in worthless Enron stock. This heavy concentration of ownership resulted from matching contributions being made in company stock and plan restrictions limiting participants' rights to dispose of their Enron holdings and move their money into other plan investment funds. These restrictions have now been liberalized by the Pension Protection Act of 2006 (PPA) so that participants can, at any time, diversify company stock owned as a result of their own contributions and diversify company stock owned as a result of employer contributions, once a participant is credited with three years of service under the plan.

There has been a lot of fiduciary breach litigation over the use of company stock as an investment option, generally occasioned by significant drops in company stock prices and allegations that plan fiduciaries failed to take action which would have avoided or limited resulting participant losses. Such allegations invariably concerned what plan fiduciaries knew, or should have known, about the employer's business and the circumstances leading to the drop in stock price. In response, many courts developed a theory that plan fiduciaries enjoyed a "presumption of prudence" and, as a result, the majority of claims failed.

Recently, however, the U.S. Supreme Court determined that ERISA permitted no such presumption, theoretically making it easier for such claims to prevail in the future.[28] However, the Court also said that fiduciary duties do not require a fiduciary to breach securities laws. Accordingly, a claim will not prevail if it alleges that plan fiduciaries failed to act in the best interests of participants when they could have done so based on non-public information in their possession. In other words, participants can't look to plan fiduciaries to protect their interests if taking such action would require use of inside information.

According to 401(k)helpcenter.com[29], only 18.2% of 401(k) plans allow company stock as an investment option for both participants and employer contributions. 3% of plans allow company stock as an investment option for employer contributions only.

So, there are fewer plans today that allow company stock, and that is probably a good thing. Although owning company stock through your 401(k) plan has tax advantages, such ownership deprives you of the ability to achieve broad investment diversification and, if the stock tanks, you lose not only your money but your job. Ask yourself: is that a risk worth taking?

2. How employer contributions work

When you enroll as a 401(k) plan participant, you must sign a deferral election indicating the percentage of compensation that you wish to contribute to your plan. This contribution reduces your taxable income and you pay no tax on the accumulated contributions and investment earnings until you withdraw the money from the plan without rolling it over to another 401(k) plan or to an IRA.

As mentioned in the Introduction, the earlier in your career that you start contributing, the greater will be your wealth accumulation and ability to achieve a secure retirement income. However, bear in mind that, through plan design, your employer may limit the amount you may defer and, as we saw earlier, there are IRS limits on contributions as well.

What can significantly enhance your retirement income prospects is the availability of employer contributions. These can be in the form of matching contributions or discretionary/profit sharing contributions, depending on how your employer has designed the plan.

Matching contributions are the most common form of employer contributions and some form of match is offered by the vast majority of 401(k) plans.[30] The match will generally be in the form of a percentage of your contributions. The most common formula is $0.50 per $1.00 of pay up to 6%.[31] An alternative would be $1.00 per $1.00 of pay up to a different specified percentage of pay.

A discretionary or profit sharing contribution is an employer contribution that is allocated on the basis of compensation and it can go to employees even if they don't participate in the plan.

From a retirement readiness perspective, you should regard your employer matching contribution as *"free money"* and contribute sufficiently enough to your plan to take full advantage of the employer match.

3. How eligibility and vesting provisions work

Employers determine when you can join the 401(k) plan by adopting plan provisions dealing with eligibility. According to 401(k)helpcenter.com, 62% of 401(k) plans allow employees to begin contributing immediately upon becoming employed. 46.2% of employers that provide matching contributions allow immediate eligibility to receive the match, while 29.4% require one year of service prior to becoming eligible to receive it.

Once eligible, the big question is when do contributions become yours? Put another way, if you leave your employment before retirement, can you take with you what's in your account? The answer depends on what the plan says about "vesting", i.e. the process of acquiring ownership.

First, you are always fully vested in your own contributions and the investment earnings attributable to those contributions. However, when it comes to employer contributions, your rights may be different because your employer can effectively place strings on those rights, generally in the form of graduated vesting based on years of service. For example, the plan may provide that you become vested each year in 20% of your employer contributions and earnings, so that at the end of five years you are fully vested. The alternative to graduated vesting is called "cliff" vesting, where, for example, you have no entitlement for two years but at the end of that period you become fully vested. Under government regulation, the plan must provide 100% vesting at the end of six years, unless the plan provides for cliff vesting when you must become 100% vested at the end of three years of participation in the plan.

According to 401(k)helpcenter.com, 46% of employers allow immediate vesting in employer contributions and the majority of the remainder have graduated vesting. You can use these benchmarks to compare what occurs in your plan in terms of eligibility and vesting.

4. Employer responsibilities

Employers who offer company stock as an investment option today are faced with a number of issues based on the fiduciary duties of loyalty and care owed to you and the other participants in your plan. As with other investments, the IPS established by the employer should have provisions dealing with company stock. For example, the IPS should state the purpose for including company stock as an investment option under the plan and the criteria and benchmarks that will be applied when monitoring and evaluating investment performance. The IPS should also contain a provision describing the process that will be followed to protect the interests of participants, for example if the company would be subject to a takeover or to a precipitous drop in stock price. Having established these provisions, your employer should include company stock as an agenda item for meetings of the plan's investment committee.

Cautious employers will conclude, as a result of the U.S. Supreme Court decision referred to above, that use of nonpublic business information in making decisions for the benefit of participants about company stock potentially poses a conflict of interest. This is because the securities laws prevent the disclosure to participants of the employer's nonpublic business information which, as a fiduciary to the plan, the employer is otherwise compelled to disclose in order that participants may act to protect their interests. Some employers will try to eliminate this risk by populating the investment committee with staff members who are not privy to inside information, but it is difficult to see how this protects the employer when the board of the employer, presumably in possession of inside information, is to perform fiduciary oversight of the investment committee's activities.

The practical answer for the employer is to appoint an independent fiduciary to manage the company stock fund on behalf of the plan. The independent fiduciary would not be privy to inside information and would make any assessment of the company stock based only on publicly available information.

Many Employers have decided to drop the company stock fund from their plans in recent years. Certainly the U.S. Supreme Court decision will change the way employers view their company stock fund and it would be prudent for employers to undertake a review of their company stock fund arrangements.

Leaving the topic of company stock, there are a number of functions performed by an employer which are not considered to be fiduciary functions. These would include the decision to adopt the 401(k) plan and how the plan and its benefits are to be structured. These are considered to be business decisions. Accordingly, the decision to offer a matching contribution and how much the match should be are business decisions not subject to a fiduciary standard of care, even though there are limits imposed on contributions by regulation. The same would be true for decisions regarding eligibility and vesting.

5. Questions to ask your employer

There are few questions that you may ask your employer about eligibility and vesting since these are matters of plan design for your employer to decide for business reasons. The same is true about contributions, although if your plan does not offer a match there is no reason why you cannot ask what circumstances would be required for your employer to change its position.

Assuming company stock is an available plan investment option, you could ask the following questions:

1. How was the decision made to include company stock as an investment option in our plan?
2. What evaluation of the company stock fund is performed for the benefit of participants?
3. What criteria are applied in such evaluation?
4. How often is an evaluation performed?
5. Has an evaluation of the company stock fund been performed as a result of the U.S. Supreme Court decision in Fifth Third Bancorp v. Dudenhoeffer?
6. What conclusions and decisions resulted from such evaluation?

7. Has an independent fiduciary been appointed to look after the participants' interests in the company stock fund?

8. If not, to what extent will nonpublic information be used to protect the interests of plan participants who are invested in the company stock fund?

[28] *Fifth Third Bancorp v. Dudenhoeffer*, No. 12-751, June 25, 2014

[29] *Benchmark Your 401(k) Plan – 2015.* http://www.40khelpcenter.com/benchmarking.html

[30] According to Deloitte who conducted an online survey of 265 employers, ranging in size from under 100 employees to more than 10,000 employees, 96% were offering some form of matching or profit sharing contribution. *Annual Defined Contribution Benchmarking Survey, 2013-2014 Edition, Deloitte.*

[31] *Benchmark Your 401(k) Plan – 2015.* http://www.40khelpcenter.com/benchmarking.html

Chapter 7: Summary of Employer Fiduciary Responsibilities

What you will learn:

1. **It's about the Process!**
2. **The Fiduciary Framework**
3. **Employers must know what constitutes a "fiduciary"**
4. **Role of Plan Administrator**
5. **Prohibited Transactions**
6. **Exclusions from employer's fiduciary functions**

Introduction

Throughout this guide we have talked about the fiduciary responsibilities of employers in managing a 401(k) plan and the investment process. For convenience, we summarize those responsibilities here. An important starting point is that much of an employer's fiduciary responsibilities is about "process". This means that employers are expected to follow a "prudent process" when making decisions about investments and plan management. Such a process requires a diligent investigation and evaluation, so that a resulting decision is both informed and reasoned. However, a prudent process will not excuse a patently imprudent decision. For example, if the IPS does not identify "emerging markets" as a permitted fund category, the subsequent inclusion of an emerging markets fund would likely be found to be imprudent.

1. It's about the Process!

Employers must:

- Know the Fiduciary Framework

- Know What Constitutes being a "Fiduciary"

- Know what are the Fiduciary Duties

- Have a Written Fiduciary Plan – Investment Policy Statement ("IPS")

- Make Informed and Reasoned Decisions to achieve appropriate outcomes

- Pay only reasonable costs

- Document All Decisions

However:

- Fiduciaries Are Not the Guarantors of Investment Returns!

- Fiduciaries Are Not the Guarantors of the Lowest Plan Costs!

2. The Fiduciary Framework

The elements of the Fiduciary Framework are:

- Employee Retirement Income Security Act of 1974 ("ERISA")

    ✓ Under ERISA, the IRS establishes qualification rules governing tax treatment for employers and participants

    ✓ Under ERISA, the DOL is responsible for fiduciary matters and prosecuting misuse of plan assets

- Plan Document – this sets forth the terms of the plan

- Summary Plan Description (SPD) – this summary is for distribution to participants and describes important plan provisions and the rights of participants

- Trust Agreement – every plan must have its assets held in trust for participants and beneficiaries

- IPS – the investment roadmap

- Board and investment committee minutes and documents – the board and investment committee should keep minutes of meeting dealing with plan related matters and retain supporting documents

- Participant Disclosures – ERISA requires quarterly and annual disclosures to participants

3. **Employers must know what constitutes a "fiduciary"**

- A person is a fiduciary "to the extent" he or she:

    - Exercises discretion or control over the management or administration of the plan or the management or disposition of plan assets;

    - Renders investment advice for a fee or other compensation; and

    - Has any discretionary authority or responsibility in the administration of a plan.

- Who is included?

    - Look at function, not form or title

    - Likely to include: Corporate Officers (e.g. CEO,CFO, HR Director), Investment Committee Members, Trustee, Plan Sponsor (Employer),

Plan Administrator, Investment Advisor to the plan

- The employer, if named as the plan administrator, or if the Board of Directors retains oversight responsibility

4. Employers must know the fiduciary duties

- Execute responsibilities with the care, prudence skill and diligence of a "Prudent Expert" (duty of care)

- Act solely in best interests of participants and beneficiaries and avoid conflicts of interest (duty of loyalty)

- Hold and deal with plan assets for the exclusive purpose of providing plan benefits and defraying reasonable expenses of administering the plan (exclusive benefit rule)

- Follow plan documents

- Select diverse range of investments

- Pay only reasonable costs

- Avoid Prohibited Transactions

- Be bonded against theft

5. Role of Plan Administrator, usually the employer

- Selects service providers, including investment advisor to plan

- Responsible for government reporting

- Responsible for participant disclosures

- Functions are fiduciary in nature

6. Prohibited Transactions

- ERISA prohibits the furnishing of goods and services between the plan and an interested party, e.g. the employer

- Prohibited transactions Include a loan between the plan and a party in interest

- The employer's failure to make timely contributions constitutes a prohibited loan by the plan to the employer

7. Business decisions excluded from employer's fiduciary functions

- Plan design, including plan eligibility and formulation of benefits

- Making plan amendments and plan termination

Summary of Employer Fiduciary Responsibilities

Know the Process

Know the Fiduciary Framework

Know what Constitutes a "Fiduciary"

Know the Fiduciary Duties

Know the Role of Plan Administrator, usually the Employer

Avoid Prohibited Transactions

Seperate Business Decisions from Fiduciary Functions

Conclusion to Part 1

The purpose of the first half of this guide has been to improve the knowledge base of 401(k) plan participants about the architecture of 401(k) plans and the decision making process and responsibilities of employers.

As you will have gleaned from what you have read, we believe that lack of transparency as to how employers manage the company 401(k) plan is an unnecessary impediment to participants making informed investment decisions with respect to their accounts.

Why does this lack of transparency exist? The answer is simple.

As 401(k) plans have evolved, employers have limited their disclosures to what is specifically mandated by ERISA. No doubt, they have been encouraged to adopt this limited view by service providers and by their attorneys, apparently without any regard to whether increased transparency would potentially improve participant outcomes.

Some will argue that, in establishing ERISA, Congress desired to strike a balance between the needs of protecting retirement plan participants and not making the law so onerous that it would discourage employers from adopting retirement plans. Therefore, they will argue that the burden on employers that would be created by increased disclosures would be too onerous. Others will point to court decisions where access to additional disclosures was denied.

As stated in the Introduction, this guide is not a legal treatise. Its authors are not practicing attorneys and they are not calling for more regulation. On the other hand, providing the greater transparency advocated in this guide does represent a practice which we hope prudent employers will adopt.

This makes eminent sense irrespective of the law. However, referring back to the Introduction, there is legal authority to justify such requests when one looks at the law of trusts.

So, let's turn to the practical aspects of what we propose.

First, it should be recognized that, while some 401(k) plans suffer from benign neglect by management focused on other priorities, and some are mismanaged, as evidenced by DOL enforcement action and fiduciary breach litigation, the vast majority of employers are dedicated to helping their employees create a positive retirement savings outcome.

Accordingly, when asking employers questions posed by this guide, which some may regard as unconventional, it may be helpful, first, to acknowledge to your employer that you appreciate their efforts to offer a top quality plan.

If then asked why you need the information you are requesting, you can respond that the information is reasonably necessary for you to evaluate the quality of the plan and to make informed investment decisions. An employer may be surprised by some questions, but there should be no reason why an employer who wants to help participants make sound decisions would refuse a request.

If, after reasonable efforts, your employer refuses your request, you should review the Summary Plan Description provided by your employer, particularly the section entitled "Your rights under ERISA". This section will direct you to the DOL's Employee Benefits Security Administration ("EBSA"), either the local office or the office in Washington, DC. You may request assistance from EBSA by completing an online Request for Assistance, which can be found at: https://www.askebsa.dol.gov/WebIntake/Home.aspx. When completing the form, you can check the box for "Plan Operation" and explain your request in the Comments box.

Much has been written about litigation risk that employers face as sponsors of 401(k) plans.[32] We regard litigation to compel disclosure to be counterproductive and too costly. So, what then to do?

If an employer should be reluctant to comply with your request for information, you should ask your employer whether, as an alternative, your employer would agree to an independent audit of the plan's conformity with fiduciary best practices.

While this will not provide you with access to what you have requested, such an audit will address the majority of the issues covered in this part of the guide and, assuming a positive outcome, you will know that an expert has found that the decisions made by your employer, regarding investments, conform to a fiduciary standard of care, and that such expert has also identified opportunities, where they exist, for improving the investment process. Such an audit will also benefit the other participants in the plan, as well as management and the business owners.[33]

---

[32] See for example *401(k) Litigation: The 'Next Asbestos'?* and Retirement Income Journal, March 26, 2013

[33] There are many professional firms who conduct ERISA and investment audits. The Centre for Fiduciary Excellence - CEFEX, for whom one of us, Roger Levy, acts as an Analyst, conducts fiduciary audits based on well-established Prudent Investment Practices. Since any audit will benefit the employer as well as others, the cost should be borne by the employer.

Chapter 8: Personal Financial Planning Viewpoint for 401(k) Decisions

What you will learn:

1. **What is financial planning and how does it impact your 401(k) plan?**
2. **Budgeting and the importance of cash reserves**
3. **Risk management as part of your financial plan**
4. **Retirement planning and the role of employer sponsored retirement plans**
5. **Investment planning and management**
6. **Other financial planning areas**
7. **Your employers' responsibilities**
8. **Questions to ask your employer**

1. What is financial planning and how does it impact your 401(k) plan?

This guide pertains primarily to 401(k) plans, which are a tool to accumulate capital as part of your retirement planning, so that you can generate income to replace your paycheck. However, retirement planning is only one part of overall financial planning. In order to give you an understanding of how your retirement planning impacts your overall financial plan and to provide context for your 401(k) plan, this chapter is devoted to reviewing the basic components of financial planning as a framework for financial security. According to the Certified Financial Planner Board of Standards, Inc.[34], financial planning refers to "the process of determining whether and how an individual can meet life goals through the proper management of financial resources."

The main areas of personal financial planning, according to the American Institute of Certified Public Accountants[35], include cash flow planning, risk management, retirement planning, investment planning, estate planning, elder planning, charitable planning, education planning, and tax planning. While the purpose of a 401(k) plan is to provide income for a comfortable retirement, one must consider certain issues within one's overall financial planning in conjunction with the decision to participate in the company's 401(k) plan. A benefit of comprehensive financial planning is that it allows for better decisions to be made on the individual parts of personal wealth management, such as your 401(k) plan.

Many companies that provide 401(k) plans for their employees also provide financial planning sessions or resources to assist the individual to understand and implement the aspects of good financial planning. You are encouraged to use the financial planning related resources that your employer provides you, as well as other available resources. Each of the main areas of personal financial planning will be reviewed briefly in order for an individual to build a foundation and context for decisions more specific to their 401(k) plan decisions.

Main Areas of Personal Financial Planning

Cash Flow Planning	◆	Elder Planning
Risk Management	◆	Charitable Planning
Retirement Planning	◆	Education Planning
Investment Planning	◆	Tax Planning
Estate Planning	◆	Miscellaneous Planning

2. Budgeting and the importance of cash reserves

Cash flow planning, or what may be referred to as personal budgeting, serves as the beginning of obtaining a grip on an individual's financial situation. While many individuals resist the constraints and controls of a budget, a good budget will provide you a clear picture of where your cash flow is coming from and where it is going. This allows for smarter decisions and strength when one is tempted by issues such as impulse spending.

It is important to note that participation in a 401(k) plan normally involves forgoing some of your paycheck cash flow, as it is instead contributed to your 401(k) retirement account. While the actual cash flow impact of contributing to your 401(k) plan may be lessened because of income tax savings, your net paycheck will be smaller nevertheless. A general viewpoint is to contribute an amount to your 401(k) plan that will trigger the maximum employer match provisions, as this is, in essence, "free money" for you. However, budgeting and cash flow effects must be considered when you participate in a 401(k) plan.

In tandem with budgeting and cash flow evaluation, individuals should try to build cash reserves. The purpose of a cash reserve is to meet unexpected and urgent short term cash needs. It is generally suggested that your cash reserves be in safe and easy-to-access investments, such as money market, CDs, savings accounts, and U.S. Treasury bills. Many financial planners recommend that you generally have cash reserves reflecting 3-6 months of your regular living expenses.[36]

While cash reserves should be your primary source, you may be able to tap available credit, such as a home equity line for emergencies as well, but such short term borrowings should serve as a secondary source. Many 401(k) plans allow a participant to either borrow funds from their account or allow for hardship distributions for items such as medical or funeral expenses, which may serve as a third level of potential cash reserves. It can be helpful for you to identify and list the potential sources of cash resources, which you have access to before a need arises. A portion of every personal budget should be allocated to building a comfortable level of cash reserves.

3. Risk management as part of your financial plan

Risk management looks to prepare for potential risks in order to minimize financial loss. One must evaluate risks based on personal lifestyle and background. The first step in risk management is to identify the potential events or risks that could have a material impact on your financial resources and evaluate alternatives to reduce those risks and related losses from those events. For example, when we look at the risk of premature death and the loss of income from the wage earner, there are two broad approaches to follow. First, we can reduce the risk of premature death by living a healthy lifestyle, perhaps by engaging in a better diet and exercise routine. The second approach is to reduce the financial loss from the premature death event by obtaining life insurance. Of course, the prudent approach tells us to do both. It is common and easy to think of insurance (life, health, disability, property & casualty, etc.) as the way to reduce financial risk, but it is just as important to implement changes to behavior and the condition of property through adequate repairs and maintenance to reduce the potential for events that cause negative financial consequences.

Another risk reduction technique that anyone can use is to properly document information, which may help you or a family member in the occurrence of an emergency or negative event. This includes information about your 401(k) plan, as well as other company-provided employee benefits. There are many resources that provide specific solutions for identified risks and are beyond the scope of this work. However, the process of identifying possible risks and potential solutions that can reduce any negative financial impact is the key to proper risk management. Your employer may offer many forms of risk management solutions in the way of insurance programs as well as education and lifestyle change assistance.

4. Retirement planning and the role of company-sponsored retirement plans

Retirement planning involves preparing for your retirement in both the pre-retirement years, when you are accumulating capital wealth, as well as the post retirement years when you are reducing or living off of that wealth. There are both financial and non-financial considerations that are equally important. The objective is to identify and implement strategies that increase the success rate of meeting your retirement goals, and so it begins with goals that relate to personal budgeting. What kind of lifestyle do you want to have in retirement and what will be the cost? Once your lifestyle costs are understood, you can identify the financial resources to meet those costs. The shortfall which must be funded can be determined by subtracting the required financial resources for retirement from your current financial resources. This type of analysis provides insight into whether you are on the right track in terms of saving enough for your retirement.

Generally, the best way and order to fund your retirement, assuming you have adequate cash reserves, is by (1) contributing to your 401(k) plan up to the amount that the employer will match, (2) contributing the maximum to a Roth IRA if eligible, (3) contributing to your 401(k) up to the remaining limit, and (4) invest in marketable securities, such as stocks, bonds, and mutual funds in a regular taxable account. For some individuals, it may be appropriate to add deferred annuities and other types of investments. The earlier you start saving for retirement, the better your chances of accumulating the necessary wealth to fund a comfortable retirement.

When it comes to using funds in retirement, individuals can use a combination of social security income, pensions, 401(K) plans, IRAs and personal investments as the source of retirement funds. The decision as to what sources to use and when depends on cash flow needs, both currently and in the future years of retirement, as well as tax considerations, which will be addressed in a separate chapter. How much cash flow an individual needs from their various retirement fund sources can vary each year. In addition, based on their individual tax situation and other financial planning goals, the specific combination and appropriate amounts from each source will vary as well.

Some individuals will consider their personal residence as an asset available to meet their projected retirement costs, but some will not since they wish to live in their home for the remainder of their life without any related mortgage. There are ways to tap the capital from your personal residence, including outright sale, mortgage or home equity line, or reverse mortgage. One should be cautious when considering tapping into the value of their personal home to fund retirement, and such decisions should be made with advice from knowledgeable individuals who will consider the long term impact.

For many individuals, employer sponsored retirement plans will be a significant portion of their wealth and will serve as a primary source of retirement income. In some cases, the employer may sponsor a defined benefit pension plan, which has the objective of providing a specific stream of income throughout the retirement years, many times based on a percentage of average salary for the final years. In some cases, the employer may sponsor a defined contribution plan, whereby funds will be contributed into the plan by either the employer or employee. The actual accumulated value will determine how much is available to the employee. Examples of defined contribution plans include 401(k) and 403(b) retirement plans. In some cases, the employer may sponsor and make available both types of plans.

Another consideration, which applies to both the defined benefit pension and defined contribution retirement plans, is how much, if any, the employer will contribute to the retirement plan versus the funds contributed by the individual directly through payroll withholding. In many cases, the employer will match a certain percentage of the employee's contribution to encourage participation. For example, the employer may match 50% up to 6% of employee's compensation, which means that if the employee elects to defer 8% of their compensation into the 401(k) plan, the employer will match 50% up to 6%, which equals 3% of that employee's compensation contributed by the employer on behalf of that employee. In addition, there may be vesting requirements that limit the amount related to the employer's contribution into your account that you are entitled to if you leave the employer before a certain number of years. Many of these retirement plan specific issues are covered in more detail in other chapters of this guide. As part of your overall financial planning, it is important for you to understand how your employer-sponsored retirement plan will impact your overall financial goals, and for you to know what kind of plan(s) your employer has available to you and how they function.

5. Investment planning and management

Investment planning begins with understanding your purpose for investing. Secondly, you need to decide how much you can afford to invest and how often. The third basic variable is your timeframe and when you will need the funds from your investments. Based on these first three answers, you can decide how much risk you should take with your investments. Finally, the last part of the investment management decision is the selection in what you should invest. Many individuals pick their specific investments without going through all of these steps and they end up with a mixture of investments with no relation to the underlying purpose for investing in the first place. Once you make your investment decision, you should monitor and adjust your allocation of investments based on your changing risk tolerance and ongoing market conditions. This process should be implemented for both retirement plan investments as well as personally held investments, and the overall investment management process should factor in all of an individual's investments, both inside and outside of retirement plan accounts. In regard to your 401(k) plan, this guide devotes an entire chapter toward personal investment planning and management decisions. See Chapter 10.

6. Other financial planning areas

There are other areas of financial planning that you need to consider in order to properly manage the decisions involving your 401(k) plan. While not all-inclusive, some of these areas include tax planning, estate planning, elder-care planning, charitable giving, and education planning. For example, when you contribute part of your compensation to a 401(k) account, that amount is not taxable for federal income tax purposes, in essence you receive a deduction for your contribution, which will save you income tax. The areas of tax and estate planning aspects will be covered in Chapter 9. Many of these topics are beyond the scope of this guide and will only apply to certain individuals. There are many options available for individuals to engage in financial planning. There may be resources available from your employer, on the internet and at public libraries.

You may wish to work with a professional financial planner to help you with your financial planning. When working with a professional financial planner, you want to know how they earn their income. For example, do they earn commissions on the investments or insurance products they provide you with, as this may result in a bias for recommendations. You may wish to obtain in writing that your financial planner will be acting as a fiduciary for you. A fiduciary places their clients' interests first and foremost, and must act accordingly. In addition, you want to research your financial planner's education, credentials, and experience. If your financial planner offers investments, you can go to www.sec.gov and see their ADV form and brochure, which provides extensive information about your financial planner and their firm. You may want to visit the following site, http://www.finra.org/investors/professional-designations to view a listing of professional financial credentials and their related websites where you can find additional information. If you establish a relationship with a financial professional, you want to do your homework so you will have a long-term partner that will be a positive force to help you accomplish your financial goals.

7. Your employer's responsibilities

While the degree of responsibility and actions taken by your employer may vary based on their philosophy and culture, there are certain aspects of employee benefits regulated by law and governmental agencies in order to protect you. For example, the Employee Retirement Income Security Act (ERISA)[37] was established to set minimum standards and to protect the interest of participants in employee benefit plans. Both the Department of Labor (DOL) and the Internal Revenue Service (IRS) are governmental agencies that enforce the provisions of ERISA. In addition, there are best practices and resources available to any employer if they wish to improve the quality of experience their employees receive through the various employee benefits offered. Many of the specific provisions of ERISA and other standards, which impact employer-sponsored retirement plans, are covered at length in the earlier chapters of this guide. The authors of this guide believe that support from your employer shows moral responsibility, as it is a benefit to them to have employees who are financially secure.

Questions to ask your employer

1. What financial education resources does the company provide to employees?
2. What employee benefits are available, such as insurance programs and lifestyle assistance, to employees by the company?
3. Who are the primary and contingent beneficiaries of my various company benefits?
4. What resources and education does the employer provide regarding the retirement plan?
5. Where can I learn about the specific rules, characteristics, and attributes of the company-sponsored retirement plan and what resources are available?
6. What does the company or 401(k) service provider offer in the way of both general and specific financial planning education and counseling?

[34] CFP Board. http://www.cfp.net/

[35] American Institute of Certified Public Accountants. http://www.aicpa.org

[36] Lindblad, M. (2016). *What is a Sufficient Cash Reserve?* http://finance.zacks.com/sufficient-cash-reserve-9717.html

[37] Employee Retirement Income Security Act of 1974 (ERISA), Pub. L. No. 93-406, 88 Stat. 829

Chapter 9: Personal Tax Aspects of Employer Sponsored Retirement Plans

What you will learn:

1. **The importance of tax planning**
2. **The tax impact of participating in your employer sponsored retirement plan**
3. **Regular versus Roth options**
4. **Tax planning strategies**
5. **Other tax opportunities, traps, and considerations**
6. **Your employers' responsibilities**
7. **Questions to ask your employer**

1. The importance of tax planning

Taxes are one of the largest expenditures that individuals will incur during their lifetime. There are various types of taxes used as a means for governmental units to produce revenue for the programs and services they provide. While how the government uses our tax money is usually a topic of controversy, the fact of the matter is that individuals will always have to factor taxation into their long-term financial and retirement planning. Oliver Wendell Holmes is quoted as saying "Taxes are the price we pay for civilization". [38] Some of the more common forms of taxes individuals face include income tax, sales tax, excise tax, and estate taxes, as well as penalties from the government, which maintain the characteristics of a tax. Several of these taxes are relevant to your participation in your employer-sponsored retirement plan and are worth discussing.

2. The tax impact of participating in your employer sponsored retirement plan

When an individual participates in his/her employer sponsored retirement plan, the amount contributed by both the employer and the employee results in an immediate reduction of taxes, (with the exception of Roth contributions). Your employer receives a tax deduction for employer contributions to your retirement plan, up to certain limits under IRS rules. These contributions can include matching contributions on the amount you contribute, as well as additional employer contributions, such as profit sharing. For the individual, when you elect to contribute to your 401(k) plan, the amount is withheld from your paycheck on a pre-tax basis, i.e. prior to the calculation of federal income tax. In essence, you are receiving a tax deduction for your contributed funds because those amounts are not included in your year-end W-2 form as part of taxable wages. Note that state and local governments may differ in their treatment of employee contributions to 401(k) accounts and so, while some will follow the federal treatment of 401(k) contributions, others may not allow the exclusion from your income.

The amount of potential tax savings you will receive is a factor of two variables. The first factor is how much of your salary to defer and contribute to your 401(k) plan, and the second factor is your "marginal income tax rate." When we refer to your marginal income tax rate, we are referring to the rate of income tax you would be paying on the next dollar of income or the rate of income tax savings you will receive on the next dollar of tax deduction. There is a good deal of confusion when individuals talk about their tax bracket and tax rate. For example, if you divide the amount of income tax you pay by your income amount, you have computed the average income tax rate. This is different from the marginal tax rate. What is most important for tax planning is the marginal tax rate because that will provide you the information on the tax effect of the tax planning related action you are considering. For example, if you are in the 28% marginal tax bracket and elect to defer $10,000 to your 401(k) plan, the immediate after tax cash flow cost of that contribution is $7,200, as a result of the income tax savings. Another way to look at this example is that for a current $7,200 cost, or reduction in your cash flow, you now have $10,000 working for you and accumulating for your retirement.

Another tax related phrase that produces confusion is "tax bracket." Your tax bracket is the range of income taxed at a certain marginal tax rate. For example, in 2015 a single person would pay 10% on the first $9,225 of taxable income, 15% on taxable income between $9,226 and $37,450, 25% on taxable income between $37,451 and $90,750, 28% on taxable income between $90,751 and $189,300 and 33% on taxable income in excess of $189,300. If their taxable income was $85,000, they would be considered in the 25% income tax bracket. Note that just because they are in the 25% income tax bracket, it does not mean they pay 25% on all of their taxable income. They actually will pay 10% or 15% on some taxable income and 25% on only the taxable income above $37,451. Sometimes individuals are confused to the point that they may misinterpret the benefit and tax impact of getting a bonus because it will throw them into a higher tax bracket and they believe they will end up paying the higher tax rate on all their wage income. So, in our example, if we add a $10,000 bonus to the $85,000 salary and raise the taxable income to $95,000, the new tax bracket and marginal tax rate would be 28%. Note that the result is that only the taxable income above $90,750 is taxed at the rate of 28% and the bonus had no effect on the tax rate of the remaining taxable income. Another way to put this is that if you are faced with the decision to take the bonus or forfeit it, regardless of tax consequences, you should take it! Perhaps when faced with the decision of how much to defer to your 401(k) plan you may wish to consider how much room you have in the higher tax bracket to take advantage of higher tax savings and use that as a guideline for your contribution. When it comes to how much to contribute to your 401(k) plan, you have control over how much to defer and you need to understand what your marginal income tax rate is and how income tax brackets work, so you can make a better decision that will lead to a greater after-tax accumulation of wealth.

3. Regular (pre-tax) versus Roth options

Many employer-sponsored retirement plans offer a Roth 401(k) account option, as well as a regular 401(k) account. The primary differences between a regular 401(k) and a Roth 401(k) is the tax treatment of both contributions, as well as distributions from the plan. As previously mentioned, in a regular 401(k) plan, the amount you contribute reduces your taxable income and saves income tax for the year of contribution. When you contribute to a Roth 401(k) there is no current reduction in your income tax. However, ultimately, when you receive distributions from your Roth 401(k) plan, all distributions are tax-free. Another way to understand the differences is to look at the timing of the tax benefit and the amount to which the tax benefit applies. With a regular 401(k) plan, you receive the tax benefit in the year of contribution and you defer the tax until you receive distributions in the future. These distributions consist of both what you have contributed, as well as the investment gains while you were participating in the plan. With a Roth 401(K), you do not receive a tax benefit in the year of contribution, but you do receive a tax benefit in the future. With a Roth 401(k), both your initial contribution and all of your investment growth will be received tax-free upon withdrawal from the 401(k) plan. Note that any contributions, such as matching or additional profit sharing contributions made by your employer, are normally deposited into your regular 401(k) account. Therefore, when referring to Roth 401(k) contributions, they are typically entirely the employee's contributions.

If you do have a Roth option in your employer-sponsored retirement plan, you should consider yourself fortunate because you have more options available to fit in with your overall financial planning. You have the choice to contribute to your regular 401(k), your Roth 401(k), or any combination of both types of 401(k) accounts. In addition, you have the flexibility to change your allocations between the two options based on your marginal income tax rate and income tax bracket. For example, you may wish to contribute to your regular pre-tax 401(k) to reduce your income into a lower tax bracket or marginal tax rate and then allocate the remaining portion of your 401(k) contribution to your Roth 401(k), taking maximum advantage of reducing income subject to the higher rate of tax.

When you consider your long-term financial situation, you should try to estimate your marginal tax rate and tax bracket at different periods in your life in order to maximize the benefits of splitting your 401(k) contributions between Roth and regular accounts. For example, if you are just starting out in your career, you will typically be in a tax bracket with a low marginal tax rate, such as 10% or 15%. As you proceed in your career, and if your taxable income increases later in life, you will most likely be in a higher tax bracket with a marginal tax rate at a possible 28% or 33%. In this example, it may make sense to contribute to your Roth 401(k) in your earlier years and a regular pre-tax 401(k) in your later years to take advantage of the dynamics of your future higher marginal tax rates and greater savings of tax.

If you are projecting into your retirement years, many people will experience a dramatic decrease in taxable income, as a result of leaving the workplace, and their marginal tax rate may drop. If they received an income tax benefit at 28% or 33% when they contributed to their regular 401(k) and pay tax on the distributions in their retirement years at 10% or 15%, they have successfully used the tax system to increase their wealth. We sometimes refer to this planning technique as tax rate differential planning. As stated previously, every individual's tax situation may be unique. For some people, their marginal tax rate may not decrease in their retirement years because they continue to live the same lifestyle and require the same income from investments and retirement accumulations to maintain that lifestyle. Instead of funding their lifestyle with wage income, they fund it with their 401(k), or their IRA in the case of a rollover, so the taxable income before and after retirement remains the same. In addition, when we are planning many years ahead into retirement, we make assumptions about tax rates, which may not be valid because of potential future changes in our tax system and tax rate structure.

Another aspect to the Roth vs. regular 401(k) issue relates to tax deferral and the time value of money. It is commonly understood that a dollar today is worth more than a dollar 20 years from now, and we are not just talking about the effect of inflation. If we have a dollar today, we can invest it and receive a return for 20 years, so we should have a significantly higher amount than $1 at the end of the 20 year time period. We refer to this concept as the time value of money, and we should consider this factor when making decisions about contributing to company-sponsored retirement plans. In fact, one of the benefits of a company sponsored retirement plan is the tax deferral available. So, for example, perhaps your marginal tax rate remains constant and you remain in the same tax bracket both throughout your working career and your retirement years. You do not receive the tax rate differential benefit mentioned in the last paragraph, but if you can receive a tax benefit today and defer paying the tax to some future date, you have received a tax deferral benefit and your investment proceeds and growth can be reinvested in their entirety during the tax deferral period.

The decision of contributing to a regular 401(k) or a Roth 401(k) in many cases is not an easy one and will be covered further in the tax planning strategies section of this chapter. The first step is to identify if your employer-sponsored retirement plan offers a Roth option and what the procedures are for enrolling, if you choose to participate. If your employer does not offer a Roth 401(k) option, you may wish to ask them to consider adding it to their company-sponsored retirement plan.

4. Tax planning strategies

General Comparison of Regular vs. Roth 401(k) and IRA

Action	Regular	Roth
Contribution*	Tax Deduction	No Tax Deduction
Account Growth	Tax Deferred	Tax Free
Distribution*	Taxable	Tax Free

* Limitations and Restrictions may apply

The first step in tax planning is to understand your current marginal tax rate and tax bracket. In addition, you should try to project any future changes in your financial situation that might impact your marginal tax rate and tax bracket. Some common life events to consider include job and salary changes, marital changes, employment status changes (including retirement),

Roger Levy and Peter Roland

changes in a spouse's income, and significant inheritances, just to name a few. While the future may be hard to predict, both in terms of what your taxable income will be and at what rate that income will be taxed, in many cases individuals have some general idea, which may be helpful from a tax planning viewpoint. A factor that we have little influence on is what congress will do with our tax system and what rate structure will be in place in the future, which further highlights the need for tax planning to be an ongoing process.

The second step in tax planning is to identify available alternatives, which may positively influence the taxes you pay in the long-run. As related to this guide, participation in a 401(k) is one alternative that many individuals have available to them, so we will focus on the individual tax aspects of the decision to participate or not in your employer-sponsored retirement plan. While the amount that an individual can contribute to their 401(k) plan can vary, there are overall limitations set by the Internal Revenue Service and these limits have been changing over time, in order to take inflation into account. Currently, for 2016, the annual limitation on the amount of wages that an employee may defer into their 401(k) plan is $18,000. In addition, an individual who is age 50 or greater may contribute an additional $6,000 "catch-up" contribution. These limits do not apply to any contributions made by your employer.

The third step in tax planning is to rank your alternatives and select the choice or choices that are the best for you. In many cases, you might not have enough free cash flow to fund all the beneficial tax planning alternatives, so you must start with the best and work down until you no longer have discretionary cash flow available. For example, a common strategy for accumulating a retirement nest egg is to first fund your 401(k) up to the employer matching limit, fund a personal Roth IRA account, and then proceed with deferring as much as you can to your 401(k) plan. If you can fund both your 401(k) plan and your IRA account to the maximum amounts, and you still have discretionary cash flow available, there are many other investment alternatives available to further your financial goals. For example, there are tax deferred annuities, real estate, marketable securities, precious metals, and other investments that provide some tax benefits such as deferral of tax on gain, tax shelter through depreciation, and special lower tax rates. The tax planning process remains the same, and the third step is selecting the alternatives that have the most positive impact on your financial picture, through a ranking process, until your discretionary cash flow is used up. Of course every situation is different. For example, if your adjusted gross income is over the IRS limit, and you are participating in a company sponsored retirement plan, you generally can't contribute to a personal

Roth IRA, although there may be indirect strategies to accomplish the same end result. One such strategy could be by using a "back door" Roth IRA contribution where you fund a nondeductible IRA and immediately perform a Roth IRA conversion. Note that like any tax planning strategies, you must scrutinize your unique situation to determine what is viable. Furthermore, many of the available choices for using your cash flow may not be appropriate for you based on risk-reward, liquidity, transaction costs, and other detriments.

The fourth step in the tax planning process is implementing the alternative or alternatives that, through the ranking process, you have identified as the best for your situation. In reference to your 401(k) plan, this would involve adjusting your contribution levels as well as your mix of regular versus Roth 401(k) usage, if you have that option. Tax planning is personal, as there are potentially many factors that could impact your decision regarding how much to contribute to your 401(k) plan, including human emotion and behavior. Some individuals find it difficult to contribute any amount to their 401(k) plan because they feel their budget will not absorb the contribution amount. Perhaps they may wish to start contributing a small amount, with the goal of increasing that amount every year, until they reach their desired contribution amount. It is worth repeating again that the effect on your current cash flow and personal budget of a contribution to your regular 401(k) plan is softened by the fact that you save income taxes on that amount. For example, if you elect to contribute $1,000 into your 401(k) plan and you are in the 33% bracket, the reduction in your cash flow is only ($1,000 -$330 tax savings) = $670.

The fifth step in tax planning is to monitor, review, and modify the choices you have made in the fourth step. You should be reviewing your choices to make sure they still fit your needs and are providing the benefits you anticipated. We live in a world of constant change. Not only do tax laws and rates change, but so may your personal financial situation and goals. Some of the impact of your tax planning alternatives will be influenced by investment performance, which we will cover in the next chapter. The fifth step in tax planning leads you back to step one, which should reinforce to you that tax planning is an ongoing process. You may wish to partner with a tax professional, such as a Certified Public Accountant (CPA) or attorney who specializes in taxes, to assist you. There are also many good resources and tools available from investment companies, which your employer may use for your 401(k) plan, as well as information on the internet or at your public library.

Tax Planning Process

Understand Marginal Tax Rate

Identify Alternatives

Rank Alternatives and Select

Implement Alternative Actions

Monitor, Review, and Modify

5. Other tax opportunities, traps and considerations

There are various tax opportunities and traps, as well as other considerations you should be aware of when participating in your company-sponsored retirement plan. For example, there is the Retirement Savings Contributions Credit for lower income individuals who make contributions to their IRA or 401(k) plan. This is an example of an opportunity that many people often overlook.

If your 401(k) plan offers a loan provision, where you can borrow from your own account and repay it through payroll deduction, be aware that if your employment terminates and you want to distribute the balance in your account, the remaining loan amount is not only deducted from your account balance, but is considered taxable income. This means you could be subject to a 10% premature distribution penalty, in addition to being responsible for federal income tax. If you do have a loan from your 401(k) plan and you terminate your employment, you may wish to pay off your 401(k) loan before termination to avoid these negative consequences.

If you do borrow from your 401(k) plan, the loan is usually amortized and paid back over a period of 1 to 5 years, with interest. If your employer allows, and the loan is to acquire a personal residence, the period to pay it back can be substantially longer. Under current law, the interest you pay on your 401(k) loan is generally not tax deductible (unless you qualify under the investment interest deduction rules). However, if your loan qualifies, and your employer is willing to structure the loan as a mortgage on your personal residence, the interest may be tax deductible as mortgage interest on the employee's individual tax return. This additional tax benefit should be weighed against the fact that you do have an additional lien on your property, which could be enforced in the event of nonpayment of the loan. In addition, the additional lien may make it more difficult to refinance the property, which is why this alternative should only be undertaken after receiving counsel from a professional who can make you aware of all the factors that could affect you.

A potential tax trap involves any early retirement withdrawals from your 401(k) plan. For a regular 401(k), in addition to being taxed on distributions, if you are not over the age of 55 by the end of the year in which you leave and are separated from service, you will be subject to the 10% IRS penalty. A common technique, to both defer the tax on your 401(k) distribution and avoid the 10% early withdrawal penalty, is to roll your 401(k) directly into an individual retirement account (IRA account). In many cases, the proceeds from your 401(k) account are transferred directly to your IRA account, by what is referred to as a trustee to trustee transfer, and there is no taxable event upon such transfer. If you receive the proceeds from your 401(k) personally, you do have 60 days to complete a rollover into your IRA account. However, in many cases your employer will withhold 20% federal income tax on the distribution, which means you will have to make up the difference if you want to achieve a 100% tax deferred rollover. In addition, the penalty for not accomplishing the rollover in that 60 day period is 10% of the 401(k) distribution amount. If you have after tax contributions in your company sponsored retirement account, you have the option to roll over that amount into a Roth IRA. You can also convert a regular IRA to a Roth IRA but will have to pay income taxes on the conversion amount.

Estate tax and planning involves the transfer of wealth upon the death of an individual. Note that upon death your assets will pass one of three ways. The first is by ownership, such as joint tenancy with right of survivorship, typical in a personal residence owned by a married couple. With this type of ownership, the asset will pass directly to the other spouse based on how the property was titled. The second way of passing wealth is through contract agreement. This type of transfer is typically used in life insurance and is used in your 401(k) plan. The proceeds of your 401(k) account will go to the named beneficiary, or beneficiaries, as specified in the plan's related documents you have signed. In addition to beneficiaries, there are contingent beneficiaries who take the place of beneficiaries in the event the original beneficiaries are no longer living. The third way of asset transfer is by your will, which serves as a basket to catch all the assets that do not transfer by ownership title or contract agreement. It is important to understand these basics of estate planning. When it comes to your 401(k) account, you need to make sure that you are aware of your named beneficiaries and that the plan documents are up to date with your wishes. Many people revise their wills to reflect changes in their wishes but forget about changing their beneficiaries on assets such as 401(k) or IRA accounts, which, by contract, override the wishes stated in the will. This discussion is merely an introduction to some of the estate planning aspects of your 401(k) plan to make you aware of the fact that it is an important and unique asset and this does not serve as legal advice. It is recommended that you bring your 401(k) plan information, including your current beneficiaries, to any financial planning or legal professional so they consider it when they offer advice.

6. Your employer's responsibilities

Your employer is responsible for making you aware of many of the tax aspects of your participation and actions related to your 401(k) plan. For example, if you leave employment and request a distribution, there will be paperwork disclosing the tax related rules and impact of your actions. Of course, it is your responsibility to read these disclosures and act accordingly. When you contribute to a regular 401(k) plan, the result will be that you pay less income tax. Your federal income tax withholding from your paycheck should drop to reflect the reduction in taxable income, as a result of your contribution. In some instances, you may find that contributing to your 401(k) plan lowers your marginal tax rate and places you in a lower tax bracket. In these cases, you may wish to consider revising the percentage of your taxable income withheld by your employer by filing a new W-4 form. If you do file a revised W-4 form to adjust the percentage withheld from your salary, it is your employer's responsibility to carry out your request.

Many employers will have tools and assistance available so you can understand the various tax implications of participation in your 401(k) plan. For example, your employer may have hired an investment company that provides a website where you calculate the effect of using a Roth 401(k) instead of a regular 401(k) on both your current and long-term wealth accumulation. Some employers will pay for financial or tax planning services for their employees as a benefit. Your employer should make you aware of any such tools and resources so you can take full advantage of them.

Questions to ask your employer:

1. What tax planning tools and resources do you make available to employees so they can make better tax-related decisions involving their 401(k) plan?

2. Where can I find a current copy of my W-4 information used to determine what percentage of my salary is withheld for federal income tax purposes, and what is the procedure to change my W-4 to adjust my federal tax withholding?

3. Does the 401(k) plan have a Roth 401(k) option available to plan participants?

4. Does the 401(k) plan allow loans, and if so, what are the interest rates and terms applied to such loans.

5. Will the 401(k) plan allow for a trustee to trustee direct rollover to my IRA account if I leave employment so I can defer federal income tax on the rolled over amount?

6. Who are the current beneficiaries and contingent beneficiaries of my 401(k) plan for my estate and tax planning purposes?

[38]*"Oliver Wendell Holmes Quotes." Quotes.net.* STANDS4 LLC, 2016. Web. 13 Mar. 2016. <http://www.quotes.net/quote/4027>.

Chapter 10: Personal Investment Management Aspects of Employer Sponsored Retirement Plans

What you will learn:

1. Investment management as part of your overall financial planning
2. General Investment characteristics and considerations
3. Marketable securities: mutual Funds, ETFs, stocks & bonds
4. Risk and reward
5. The investment policy statement
6. Diversification, asset allocation, and rebalancing
7. Placement of investments inside or outside your 401(k) plan
8. The role of retirement plan advisors and investment company-provided management tools
9. Your employers' responsibilities
10. Questions to ask your employer

1. Investment management as part of your overall financial plan

Investment management is a critical element of financial planning and should be implemented in conjunction with other areas of financial planning in order to create a plan with the greatest chance of success in meeting your goals. Investment management involves using your excess cash flow to both store it and grow it for the future through various investment alternatives. Investment management can be looked at from different levels. First, we will focus on an individual's overall personal investment picture, which includes many different types of investment options, and then we will look at investment options with a focus on marketable securities, both inside and outside your 401(k) plan. How well one understands and uses basic investment management techniques can have a significant impact on the overall results of a financial plan and reaching the desired financial goals.

2. General Investment characteristics and considerations

Investments represent the forgoing of current consumption of resources in order to accumulate wealth over time. There are many forms of investments, and each has unique aspects that should be understood before committing funds for acquiring such investments. Some of these aspects include risk and reward, liquidity, complexity, and tax consequences. While this guide has a focus on 401(k) plans, it is important to look at your overall personal investment wealth to better understand the role and proper positioning of your 401(k) plan investments.

For example, an individual's overall wealth may include any of the following:

- cash, certificates of deposit, money market accounts
- personally held stocks, stock options, bonds, mutual funds, and exchange traded funds (ETFs)
- annuities and cash value of life insurance policies
- real estate, which includes a home residence, vacation home, and investment properties
- retirement plans, such as 401(k), IRA accounts, pension plans, 403(b) plans and deferred compensation plans
- precious metals, such as gold and silver
- collectables, such as antiques and art
- business interests and direct ownership participation in activities, such as oil and gas programs

When we look more specifically at 401(k) plans in this guide, we need to put into perspective where the retirement plan investments fit in our overall wealth picture. In most cases, your 401(k) investment options will include mutual funds, ETFs, and perhaps the ability to invest in individual stocks and bonds.

3. Marketable securities: mutual Funds, ETFs, stocks & bonds

Marketable securities generally refer to investments that are liquid in nature and can be easily sold, exchanged, and converted into cash at a price determined by an efficient market. Marketable securities can be divided into two general categories consisting of stocks and bonds. Stocks, often referred to as "equities," consist of direct ownership in companies represented by shares of stock held by investors. The return to investors in stocks can consist of both capital gain as well as dividends. When stocks increase in market value, as a result of past performance and anticipated future performance, the increase in value or appreciation in excess of the price paid for the investment is referred to as capital gain. Bonds consist of debt issued by companies and government entities and provide a return to investors in the form of interest income. Two variations of stock and bond investments, which are common, are mutual funds and exchange traded funds (ETFs).

A mutual fund is an investment vehicle consisting of numerous underlying holdings. For example, a mutual fund with the objective of investing in large company stocks will typically hold 50 to 100 different individual stocks within the mutual fund. A key advantage of a mutual fund is the ability to spread investment risk over many different holdings. We generally refer to the spreading of risk among different individual holdings, or even investment categories, as diversification. There are mutual funds that invest solely in stocks or bonds, and some invest in both. You can find the objective of the mutual fund listed in the prospectus as well as information provided to investors through literature, websites, and other sources. A mutual fund will have a management team that manages the individual investment holdings within the mutual fund. Such investment management may be active, with changes made to the underlying mutual fund portfolio to take advantage of market dynamics, or the investment management may be passive, where changes to the underlying holdings of the fund are not often made, where more of an index approach is used.

In many cases, a mutual fund may consist of several investment classes of investments blended in a way to attempt to achieve a specific objective. For example, target date funds will typically have an objective of a certain target date (usually retirement age) for an individual and will invest the underlying fund investments to meet that target date objective. For example, a target date 2025 investment option in a 401(K) plan would invest funds for someone who would be retiring close to the year 2025, and while initially invested more aggressively in equities, the fund would become more conservative as it came closer to the year 2025. A controversial issue we see today is that while some target date funds invest "to retirement," some invest "through retirement." If a fund invests "to retirement," they tend to become conservative with low equity exposure close to the retirement date, with the goal of a stable value for the fund as one approaches that retirement date. If a fund invests "through retirement," they tend to invest as if an individual will retire at a target date but utilize the funds gradually over their remaining lifetime, so a longer term investment horizon is used resulting in a larger portion of the funds invested in equities, which can result in greater volatility (price fluctuation) in the fund value. See Chapter 4 for more discussion on target date funds.

A slight variation of a mutual fund investment is an exchange traded fund (ETF), which has similar diversification advantages of using many individual holdings to accomplish a specific investment objective. A key difference with an ETF is that they trade like a stock, where the price of the ETF fluctuates during the day. This differs from a mutual fund where any buying or selling of the fund is based on the end-of-day price of the underlying holdings. In addition, with an ETF, there is normally a trading cost or commission to purchase and sell ETF holdings. Mutual funds may also have commissions or trading costs associated with them. Today there are many "no-load" or "no transaction fee" mutual funds that can be bought and sold without incurring trading costs. See Chapter 2 for a more thorough discussion of investment fees.

4. Risk and reward

Understanding the risk and reward attributes of the investments you select, both inside and outside your 401(k) account, is the first necessary step in selecting the proper mixtures and amounts to allocate to the different investment classes. We will focus on marketable securities, which generally include stocks, bonds, and mutual funds, as the other types of wealth have their own unique risk and reward attributes. While it is generally understood that the greater the risk in an investment the greater the return, it is much more difficult to quantify this relationship into the future. Risk can be defined as the uncertainty of the cash flows and end value of an investment.[39] Many investors probably have no idea of the amount of risk they are taking with their current investments, and they may not even understand exactly what they are investing in. Other investors may be so adverse to risk that they do not receive adequate returns on their investments to generate the wealth required to meet their goals. While the number of investment options has increased, so has the complexity of many of those investments, so investors have many challenges in their understanding of the investment options available and their related risk and reward attributes.

Many employer sponsored retirement plans, in conjunction with investment companies, offer tools and resources for an individual plan participant to understand the risks and rewards of the investment choices offered. For example, in the case of individual mutual funds, there may be charts and graphs that show the risk potential for an individual fund. In addition, there is normally a history of past returns to provide a historical picture of the volatility of performance. Another guideline that can be used is the classification by the fund company or plan sponsor as to the level of risk attributes for the investment. For example, The Vanguard Company[40] uses fund classifications such as conservative, conservative to moderate, moderate, moderate to aggressive, and aggressive, to help individuals visualize where a particular fund is on the risk spectrum.

For many individuals, the appropriate risk reward relationship changes throughout their lifetime. For example, generally younger individuals may wish to take more risk with their retirement funds because they have a longer investment horizon than an individual who is several years away from retirement. A longer time horizon allows for the acceptance of more variability, as time should bring investment returns closer to an average that provides the proper return for the risk taken. In addition to time horizon factors, there can be other personal characteristic changes that have an impact on 401(k) investing when an overall wealth management perspective is used. For example, a large inheritance received, which dramatically increases an individuals' wealth, may allow for additional investment risk to be taken for specific investments, including a 401(K) account, because of an increase in certainty of meeting lifetime financial goals.

Roger Levy and Peter Roland

5. The investment policy statement

An investment policy is normally a written statement that formalizes both the goals and constraints of the investor. They have been traditionally used by professional advisors, foundations, retirement plans, trusts, and other institutions to articulate the desires of the governance bodies, such as board of directors and investment committees, for managing investments. A good investment policy statement will define the objectives for returns and risk, as well as constraints that may have an impact on the proper investment of funds. Some of the common constraints that may be identified include legal requirements, liquidity needs, tax aspects as well as other characteristics of funds being invested. While the appointed investment managers may actually carry out the specific investment decisions, they are guided by the framework of the formal investment policy.

While traditionally a formal investment policy statement is used at the retirement plan level, as discussed in Part 1 of this guide, similar benefits can be obtained by individuals who wish to manage their personal investments in this way. A personal financial level investment policy statement serves as a guide for investing personal wealth. One advantage of a personal investment policy is that it requires thinking and analysis for the development of personal goals, which can be done at a time when an individual has a clear and unstressed mind and is considering the impact of their investing on a long term financial plan. While an individual may work with a professional advisor for the actual investment of funds, personal development of an investment policy statement allows one to have an active role in their investment management. The personal investment policy statement also belongs to the individual and can be used throughout their lifetime and can be modified and updated regularly as conditions and life situations change.

6. Diversification, asset allocation, and rebalancing

In order to reduce risk of loss from investing, diversification and asset allocation are two important concepts which one needs to understand. Diversification involves spreading investment capital into different types of investments that will behave differently under various conditions. Asset allocation refers to what different asset classes you use for diversifying your investments. For example, asset allocation may result in spreading your marketable securities into 8 different categories, including large, mid, and small capitalization equities, international equities, short term bonds, mid-term bonds, commodities, and money market. The number of classes to use is a personal decision and there is no perfect answer. On the one hand, adding more investment categories should result in better diversification and the spreading of risk. However, this should be balanced with the added complexity that such diversification brings to the investment management process. Within most 401(k) plans, you will have a defined number of asset classes available to you that represent a broad spectrum of investment alternatives. As a second step, you most likely have the ability to select different individual mutual funds. As mentioned previously, a personal investment policy is an excellent way to define what investment categories you will use, and will serve as a framework for selecting individual funds. As discussed in Part 1 of this guide, many retirement plans provide models of asset allocation classes and recommended percentages to achieve an overall investment portfolio appropriate for your risk and reward characteristics.

7. Placement of investments inside or outside of your 401(k) plan

It is helpful to take a step back from your 401(k) plan and take a look at your overall investment picture. Based on such an overview of your defined financial goals and situation, you may want to consider which types of investments are better placed inside your 401(k) plan versus which should be held personally outside of the plan. This decision may be impacted by tax aspects as well as investment choices you have both inside and outside of your retirement plan.

Our current income tax system treats interest income differently than qualified dividends and capital gains, with interest income not qualifying for potentially lower tax rates. If the overall investment portfolio you compile dictates the use of fixed income, or bonds, then you may want to place them within your 401(k) plan, where the current income is not taxed. Then you can allocate an offsetting portion of your investments outside the plan to investments that do receive the preferential rate on dividends and capital gains. While the overall allocation of your investment "pie" remains the same, the mix of what is inside versus outside your 401(k) changes to create a more optimal income tax situation.

As a result of their size and professional investment management, 401(k) plans may have the ability to offer you mutual fund investments not available to individual investors. In addition, 401(k) plans typically use institutional level mutual funds, which can have significantly lower fees and expenses than those available to individuals using retail level investment options. These institutional level funds can save significant costs over the life of the investment, resulting in a greater accumulation within the retirement plan versus the use of retail class shares outside the plan.

Another factor in the decision of investing inside or outside your 401(k) is the fact that, under most states' bankruptcy rules, ERISA plans, such as a 401(k), are excluded from the assets available to creditors, thus giving you another aspect of protection for funds invested inside the plan. The decision as to what specific investments you should hold inside or outside your 401(k) plan should be reviewed periodically to account for changes in tax laws, as well as your overall personal investment objectives and holdings.

8. The role of retirement plan advisors and investment company-provided management tools

Many 401(k) plans provide tools you can use to help select the proper allocation and specific investment selection for your account. In many cases, these tools are developed by the investment custodians and managers, such as websites that will lead you through a formal financial management process to help you identify your risk-reward profile and lead you to the selection of specific investment options. These internet tools are usually offered at no additional cost to the employee.

Professional advisors may be provided by your employer to help you with your investment management decisions. Many individuals may have their own personal advisor who can assist with the management of their investments both within and outside your 401(k) plan. Whether an individual uses professional advisors or manages their investments on their own, it is important to coordinate the investments inside a 401(k) plan with investments held outside the plan.

In addition to investment management tools and the availability of professional advisors either by the plan sponsor or independently acquired by the individual employee, there may be packaged investment management options offered by your employer, such as target date funds and allocation funds that perform more of the investment management function for you. These types of investment options offer convenience and time savings for plan participants.

9. Your employer's responsibilities

While the degree of responsibility and actions taken by your employer may vary based on their philosophy and culture, there are certain aspects of the investment management process for which they have a responsibility to provide you the necessary information and resources needed to make informed and educated decisions related to your 401(k) plan. Most employers will offer some form of investment management education or guidance during the retirement plan enrollment process for new plan participants. The employer can delegate to a third party service provider some of the related investment decisions, such as what mutual funds should be offered in your retirement plan. However, the employer has a fiduciary duty to make the decision of which service provider to hire to perform specific services. As indicated in the landmark Tibble v. Edison, United States Supreme Court case[41], employers have a continuing duty to properly review investments in the retirement plan that they offer employees. Normally, the mutual fund offerings are evaluated at least quarterly for performance, fees, and appropriateness within the 401(k) plan. While a third party service provider may select such mutual funds, the employer, as a plan fiduciary, must make sure that a process is being followed so that on an ongoing periodic basis the funds are being monitored for inclusion in the 401(k) plan mix. The topic of your employer's responsibilities related to the investment management function in your 401(k) plan is covered in more detail in Chapter 3 of this guide.

10. Questions to ask your employer

1. What tools and resources for determining my investment allocation are available through the plan?

2. Does the 401(k) plan have a formal investment policy statement used to provide a framework for the investment functions appropriate to the plan, and is a copy of the investment policy available to plan participants?

3. What are the investment options available through the plan and how are they selected?

4. Does the plan provide any models I can use to help me diversify into various investment classes based on my risk and reward parameters?

5. If target date funds are provided, are they being invested "to retirement" or "through retirement"?

6. Where can I obtain additional information about individual investment options, such as the mutual funds offered in my plan, fees and expenses, mutual fund objectives, etc.?

7. How do I change my investment selections and how often can I change them?

8. If advisors are providing investment advice to individual plan participants, how are they compensated?

[39] Sharpe, W., Alexander, G., & Bailey, J. (1998). Investments. Prentice Hall, 6th edition.

[40] The Vanguard Company. http://vanguard.com

[41] *Tibble v. Edison, Int'l*, 135 S. Ct. 1823, (2015)

Chapter 11: Nearing Personal Retirement

What you will learn:

1. **Key considerations as you approach retirement**
2. **Data gathering**
3. **Emotional preparation**
4. **Other financial planning considerations**
5. **Your employer's responsibilities**
6. **Questions to ask your employer**

1. Key considerations as you approach retirement

Retirement is perhaps the most significant financial event for many individuals and should be planned well in advance of your retirement date. Typically, anywhere from two to five years before you retire is ideal for re-evaluating your current condition and modifying strategies that will increase your success rate in meeting retirement goals. The closer you get to your actual retirement date, the better vision you will have about your post-employment life.

Housing is a key part of your retirement decision. Housing in your retirement years may entail purchasing a second residence, relocating, or downsizing. In today's mobile society, many individuals are retiring and moving to other parts of the country to be close to family, to enjoy the benefits of desired weather, to have more convenient access to leisure activities, and to save taxes by establishing residency in a lower tax jurisdiction. In some instances, the cost of living is much lower in certain areas. This provides a more affordable retirement lifestyle. Another increasingly viable option for some people is to retire abroad, not only to enjoy a lower cost of living, but also to be able to experience rich cultural experiences. A potential housing retirement strategy is to have more than one residence in order to take advantage of some of the common relocation benefits, and have the added option of choosing and physically being where those benefits are the greatest throughout the year. Finally, some retirees wish to physically relocate with their children in the same residence structure by adding additions and performing other renovations. Family and other relationships can play a significant role in how and where you live out your retirement years. There are numerous variations on how extended families can mutually benefit by living together, but communication and planning upfront will allow for a better relationship for everybody.

Healthcare needs may require special attention in addition to making sure you have the ability to pay for it through insurance, Medicare, and personal savings. According to HealthView Services' 2015 Retirement Care Cost Data Report[42], the average estimated future healthcare cost for a 65-year-old healthy couple will be $394,954. While some of these costs may be covered by insurance, the insurance premiums can be a significant component of related costs. Future related costs should be estimated in the preparation of retirement living costs. In addition to the financial aspect of healthcare, the coordination of health service providers is important. The pre-retirement period is a time where you want to make sure you have up-to-date medical records, histories, care providers and perhaps even prepare a formal health vision statement and plan for future health during your retirement years.

Retirement is perhaps the most significant transition in life, both financially and emotionally. The benefits of increasing the intensity of planning for your retirement event in the years near to that date will pay off throughout your retirement years. The more information and insight you obtain from others who have made the retirement journey, as well as those who have knowledge with some of the relevant issues and considerations, the better.

2. Data gathering

As you approach retirement, you want to pull together data for use in projecting your finances to assist in current decision-making processes and to prepare for the retirement transition. In addition, you want to organize financial information in the event of premature death or disability, which would require your spouse or other individuals to step into your shoes and make financial decisions. The first step in the data gathering process is to pull together your personal information, including family members, social security numbers, and birthdates, as well as contact information. The second step is to list your assets and related values, as well as ownership and any liabilities. For certain assets, such as 401(k) plans and insurance contracts, you will want to list the current beneficiary information. The third step is to estimate what your marginal tax bracket will be in the years approaching retirement, as well as after you've retired. Lastly, you want to look at and refine your personal cash flow budget to both your current pre-retirement period and post-retirement period. You should pay special attention to employee benefits and other covered expenses that may be present during the pre-retirement years and how they will change when you enter the post-retirement phase of your life.

3. Emotional preparation

While this guide focuses on the financial aspects of retirement, it is important to realize some of the emotional aspects as well. Retirement is much more than just a financial event. Retirement offers the opportunity to create a purposeful life in addition to living within your financial means. Retirement normally provides additional time for individuals to spend with family and friends, time for hobbies and leisure activities, and time to give back to society through volunteering and mentoring. It is important to realize that retirement is just a transition to a new phase of life and that you need to think about and prepare for what you are going to do in that phase. It is best to prepare well in advance of retirement. You may want to explore further the potential activities you will want to do in your retirement and start laying the groundwork for those activities. For example, if you want to become involved extensively in volunteering with a charitable organization, you may want to start with a much smaller time commitment during your pre-retirement years and ramp up that level of involvement once you retire. This will prepare you emotionally and allow you to test the waters before making a huge commitment of time when you do actually retire. While individuals are actively working, they may not have time to engage in significant social activities. A social life may be an important part of your retirement years and it can be expanded at any stage of your life, such as in the pre-retirement years.

4. Other financial planning considerations

After focusing on your personal considerations that will influence your retirement years, you want to review the financial aspects. While retirement planning finances are based on certain assumptions, it is important to test those assumptions by looking at variations in projected inflation, investment returns, and tax cash flow needs. Determine the impact these could have on your retirement and look at alternative scenarios. Your retirement phase of life can typically span for 15 to 30 years, and it is much easier to adjust your financial lifestyle from the beginning of that period instead of running into roadblocks, and even financial crises, later on in life. While in your pre-retirement years, you or a financial professional can perform projections of your cash flow needs in retirement and determine how you are going to fund those cash needs to pay for your expenses. While this process may not present you with the lifestyle scenario you desire, it does allow you to adjust your lifestyle accordingly, to have a financially comfortable retirement. Developing realistic expectations about your retirement years is a key component for success.

One area of financial planning is tax planning, which we discussed in more detail in Chapter 9. The transition from working years to retirement years may result in many individuals' tax bracket changing by becoming lower. If this is the case, there is an opportunity for multi-year tax planning by accelerating tax deductions and deferring tax income from the higher tax rate pre-retirement period to the lower tax rate retirement period. For example, additional deferral into a 401(k) plan during your pre-retirement period may make more sense, since the tax savings are higher, based on the higher tax rate. When those funds are ultimately taxable, at retirement, the individual will be in a lower tax bracket. Tax deductions, such as charitable contributions, may make sense to accelerate to the pre-retirement years because the tax savings from the charitable tax deduction will be greater in the pre-retirement years, assuming the tax rates are higher. When evaluating the pre-retirement tax rate versus retirement tax rate, the actual tax impact of acceleration or deferral of income may be impacted by social security taxation, alternative minimum taxes, and other tax issues, which involve complexity and should be planned for with a tax professional.

The other areas of your personal financial plan should be reviewed, and updated where appropriate, with a focus on identifying planning opportunities. Your insurance policies should be reviewed, along with your estate documents. As you approach the retirement date, you may wish to utilize professionals to help you with your planning, and you want to read and educate yourself as much as possible. You want to have your financial house in order before you cross that retirement starting line.

5. Your employer's responsibilities

While there is no legal mandate for your employer to provide you with specific pre-retirement assistance, many do, either directly or through the retirement plan service vendors retained by the employer. Your employer does have an obligation to provide you company-sponsored retirement plan information, such as account balances, holdings information, and retirement plan rules. In addition, the employer may have formal written policies and guidelines, which you will want to understand far in advance of your retirement date. It is recommended that you check with the human resources department at your company

6. Questions to ask your employer

1. What company-sponsored employee benefits, such as pensions or health insurance, are available to retirees?
2. What, if any, programs and support are available to retired employees of the company?
3. What is the procedure, as well as conditions, for retirement from the company?
4. Are there any other tools and resources that the employer has, or that are provided through the retirement plan service providers, to educate and help employees prepare for near term retirement?

[42] HealthView Services: 2015 Retirement Health Care Cost Report. https://www.hvsfinancial.com/PublicFiles/Data_Release.pdf

Chapter 12: Personal Retirement

What you will learn:

1. **Retirement – crossing the finish line**
2. **Budget review and update**
3. **Healthcare**
4. **Social Security**
5. **401(k) plan decisions**
6. **Your employer's responsibilities**
7. **Questions to ask your employer**

1. Retirement – crossing the finish line

Congratulations! You made it! You are retired! How does that feel? You need to visualize that moment before you get there, whether it is voluntary or involuntary retirement, to be better able to cope with that event. For many people, "retirement" from a career job may mean immediately taking on a new job, perhaps with fewer hourly requirements or less stress. For other people, retirement may mean never working for money again and spending your time on leisure or volunteer activities. And finally, for certain people, retirement is merely a frame of mind, free from financial stress, and they will choose to continue working as long as they are healthy, potentially the rest of their life. This guide, as well as the primary purpose of 401(k) plans, is to help you get to the point where you have *the option* (financially) to not work, but are still able to maintain your standard of living. What you do with your retirement will be personal and unique.

2. Budget review and update

Now that you have arrived at your retirement, it is time to adjust and evaluate your budget, for both known and estimated changes in your expenses, income, and overall cash flow. Your goal should include a plan for simplification of your finances, as well as a contingent plan for managing your finances if you ever become unable to properly perform this function. The simpler and more organized your budget and documentation are, the easier your life will be, as well as the life of your backup person (i.e. your power of attorney). Remember, the budget is a tool to provide you some degree of clarity for the future, as well as being a part of your overall financial planning, which will help you achieve your goals. It is just as important to budget when you are retired as it is in your working years. You will most likely have differences in your spending patterns, which will change and adjust to your lifestyle as you progress through your retirement years.

3. Healthcare

While many retirees rely on Medicare to pay most of their medical expenses once they reach age 65, a retiree must cover the period before that age and plan for paying the health costs not covered by Medicare. You must pay certain premiums to the government for Medicare coverage and you may wish to explore Medigap insurance to cover some of those health costs not covered by Medicare. Any premiums paid for Medicare or Medigap insurance must be considered in your budget. In addition, some individuals obtain other private health insurance, including long term care insurance, and those costs must also be considered. In some cases, the employer may provide some form of post-retirement health benefits and these should be coordinated with your human resource department.

4. Social Security

During your retirement years, social security will serve as a source of cash flow. You have the important decision to make as to when to start taking your social security. If you start taking your social security benefits before normal retirement age (currently ages 65-67 depending on your date of birth), your benefit will be smaller, but you will receive it for more years. Likewise, if you delay the date of receiving social security until after your normal retirement date, you will receive a higher payment but for fewer years. The optimal time to start taking your social security benefits will depend on how long you live, which is an unknown. However, the Social Security Administration[43] suggests you consider the following questions when making the decision:

- Are you still working? (Benefits may be reduced based on your earned income between age 62 and full retirement age.)

- Do you come from a long-lived family? (Your family life expectancy may influence your decision to start taking early, normal, or later benefits.)

- How is your health? (Your health condition will influence how many years you will be alive and collecting.)

- Will you still have health insurance? (Many people will lose their health insurance when they cease to work and Medicare usually does not start until age 65.)

- Are you eligible for benefits on someone else's record or does a family member qualify for benefits based on your record? (There are specific strategies that can maximize benefits when these types of relationships exist.)

- Do you have other income to support you if you decide to delay taking benefits? (While you may be able to optimize lifetime benefits by delaying your social security, you have to be able to live in the meantime.)

You can obtain more information at the social security website at www.socialsecurity.gov or by talking with your advisor, who can help you make these important decisions regarding collecting social security benefits. You can also visit your local social security administration office for assistance.

5. Your 401(k) specific decisions

For many individuals, their 401(k) plan represents a significant portion of their retirement capital to support them throughout their retirement years. When you leave your company, you may have various options in terms of when and how your 401(k) plan funds are distributed to you. An employee may have the option of keeping their 401(k) account in the plan and delaying distribution. While many financial professionals encourage individuals to have their 401(k) account distributed and "rolled over" to an IRA account as soon as possible, there perhaps may be some bias in such advice, as a result of the financial professional charging fees or commissions for managing those funds. In *some* cases, depending on the 401(k) plan investment platform, there may be lower cost funds available to the employee within the plan, which they will not be able to access once the 401(k) plan funds are distributed to them. Further, if you are invested in a target date fund in your 401(k) plan and intend to retain that investment beyond your retirement date, you may not want to disturb that strategy. An alternative point of view, which supports the decision to distribute the 401(k) funds and roll them into an IRA, is that the individual may have more investment options available to them than what was available within the plan, providing the benefits of diversification. The Department of Labor has recently expressed concern and focus on advisors to a company-sponsored retirement plan, such as a 401(k), who also provide advice at the individual level to an employee participant of the plan, given the potential conflict of interest. Both points of view presented should be considered by the retiring employee.

It is recommended that a retiring employee research any financial professional they might work with in order to verify their competence, experience, and any conflicts of interest. An easy way to obtain information about your investment professional is through the Securities and Exchange Commission website at www.sec.gov. Your investment professional should be listed in either the broker-dealer classification or the registered investment advisor classification. The fiduciary standard applies to registered investment advisors, which signifies they must do what is in your best interest. A suitability standard applies to broker-dealers, which requires that their recommendations must be appropriate for someone in your situation, but not necessarily be the best or least expensive in terms of fees or expenses. There are many investment professionals under both classifications that are competent and who can be an excellent resource. The choice of your investment professional may be a significant factor in the success or failure of your retirement years from a financial viewpoint. It is important to do your homework when choosing an advisor. Be sure to research their background in order to determine the appropriateness of an advisor to serve your needs.

When an employee does elect to receive their 401(k) account by distribution, it is critical that certain steps are taken to avoid the immediate taxation of the funds. The easiest way to avoid current taxation and withholding of federal income tax on your distribution is to have the funds directly "rolled over" using a trustee to trustee transfer, whereby the 401(k) account moves directly into an IRA account and the employee never has direct possession of the funds. If you take a distribution from your 401(k) and receive the funds directly, the plan sponsor must withhold 20% federal tax on such distribution and you may be subject to an early withdrawal penalty of 10% from the IRS. Both you and your employer should utilize the necessary level of care to ensure you are not hit with these potential taxes and penalties, so you receive the entire value of your 401(k) account available for investment in your IRA. Prior to rolling over your 401(k) balance to your IRA account, you want to make sure the beneficiary information for your IRA is reviewed and updated, if necessary. In addition, the investment of your IRA funds should be monitored and adjusted throughout your retirement years to match your cash flow needs and risk tolerance, and to fit your overall financial plan.

6. Your employer's responsibilities

Your employer has a responsibility to help you with your retirement transition, as it pertains to the change in your employment status and the various employee benefit plans provided. Many of these various benefit plans are regulated by government agencies, and the necessary paperwork, forms, and instructions need to be provided to you for compliance purposes. You have given your company years of service, which has benefited your company, and your company, in turn, has provided you compensation and employee benefit programs, such as a 401(k) plan, to assist you in your future retirement years. Just as important as the accumulation of funds is the transition of your funds, as well as the coordination of other benefits to which you are entitled. It should be a goal of the employer to assist with this transition to help ensure success.

7. Questions to ask your employer

1. What is the procedure to claim my company retirement plan benefits?
2. Can I stay in the 401(k) plan and any other company-sponsored plans even after I retire?
3. Can I, and how do I, roll over my company-sponsored retirement plan(s) to my IRA account?
4. Is there any post-tax money in my company-sponsored retirement plan that I can roll over to a Roth IRA?
5. Does the employer offer assistance or counseling regarding Medicare and Social Security programs for my retirement?
6. Does the company have any post-retirement health benefits and what is the procedure to claim these benefits?
7. What is the procedure for requesting that my 401(k) account proceeds are directly rolled over to an IRA via a trustee to trustee transfer in order to avoid immediate taxation?

[43]Social Security Administration. https://www.ssa.gov/

Conclusion to Part 2

The purpose of the second half of this guide has been to help prepare you for a successful personal retirement and to be able to more effectively utilize your 401(k) as a tool for that journey. In order to understand how the benefit of having a 401(k) plan can positively impact your retirement, it is critical to have an understanding of how financial planning can be used to help you achieve your goals. It is easy to become distracted by day-to-day life and push off financial planning as something you will do at a future date. Yet, that future will be here before you know it and the question you need to ask yourself is will you be ready for retirement?

In understanding financial planning as it relates to your 401(k) plan, chapters of this guide were devoted to covering the key areas of taxation and investment management considerations, both as you near retirement and when you reach the retirement finish line. These topics were introduced and reviewed at a summary level so you would have a general understanding of concepts that can make a positive difference on your retirement if they are used appropriately. Since the chapters could only provide an overview, and as there are potential complexities that could not be covered, it is recommended that you discuss these topics further with your advisor. We live in a world of constant change in tax laws, investment markets, and government regulation of retirement plans. In addition, your personal situation, desires, and goals will most likely change over time. Therefore, it is recommended that you make an effort to review your financial plan on an ongoing basis and update your specific 401(k) strategies in order to maximize benefits for your personal situation.

Part 1 of this guide provided valuable information to help you understand investment options, fees, and the responsibilities of your employer pertaining to your 401(k) plan. Part 2 provides you a framework and context for understanding how your 401(k) influences your overall financial plan and what you can do to more effectively integrate available strategies into your retirement plan. The goal of both parts of this guide is to help you understand and more effectively use your 401(k) plan, as well as to more productively work with your employer to achieve your retirement goals.

You are fortunate to have an option to participate in a 401(k) plan, as provided by your employer. You are not alone in your desire to reach your retirement goals. Throughout this guide, at the end of each chapter, there is a listing of both employer responsibilities as well as questions you should be asking your employer. We strongly suggest you to take action by encouraging your employer to understand and live up to their responsibilities to help you achieve a successful retirement.

Message to Employers:

In some sense, this guide represents a gathering storm.

The "Danger Within" for participants in your 401(k) plan is that there is a black hole in critical parts of their understanding. The purpose of this guide is to help them fill this hole, hopefully, with your help.

The black hole is how you manage the investment process. That is not to say that you are falling down on your responsibilities as they are currently understood. It is to say that your plan participants do not understand how the investments in your plan are selected and monitored, or how you evaluate and approve the investment and administration expenses that are, most typically, passed on to them. We believe that participants are entitled to this information and that as fiduciaries you are bound to supply it, just as if you were trustees of a trust established for their benefit, which is tantamount to the role you play as fiduciaries on behalf of your 401(k) plan.

While this guide may seem disruptive, it is fair to say that a more transparent environment surrounding your prudent investment process would promote more trust in your company among your employees and may even promote increased participation in your 401(k) plan. Indeed, such an environment would likely result in less fiduciary breach litigation and fewer investigations by the U.S Department of Labor.

Think of your current process this way. You want your employees to enroll in the company 401(k) plan and, through your service providers, you typically explain to them the benefits of participation and the funds that are available for investment of their contributions and of your company contributions, assuming you provide a match. But do you explain how and why you selected the particular funds or how you approved the expenses and the method of payment? As potential investors in the plan you have established, are not employees better equipped to evaluate the plan as an investment vehicle when they understand and appreciate the due diligence you have performed on their behalf in making a careful selection of the plan investments and establishing a reasonable cost and payment method?

And, on an ongoing basis, in their capacity as investors, would not participants be encouraged to maintain their participation and, perhaps, increase their contributions, if they knew the due diligence you continue to apply as the plan matures and as you anticipate change in long term market expectations?

And what of preparation for your employees' retirement? Are you proactive in helping participants nearing retirement to know what the company makes available by way of benefits and continued participation in the 401(k) plan or what steps they must take to rollover their investments elsewhere? Do you provide counseling regarding Medicare and Social Security? Do you provide adequate transparency on these matters?

It is a fact of life today that working careers will last longer. Therefore, improved transparency in relation to the matters discussed here is an imperative for both employer and employee. We hope that employers will make the effort to respond positively to questions from employees that may result from their reading this guide and to reasonable opportunities for improvement that may emerge. In the long run, we will all be better off if you do.